Milton's Unchanging Mind

Kennikat Press
National University Publications
Series in Literary Criticism

General Editor
Eugene Goodheart
Professor of Literature, Massachusetts Institute of Technology

EDWARD LeCOMTE

Milton's Unchanging Mind

Three Essays

Foreword by Douglas Bush

National University Publications
KENNIKAT PRESS • 1973
Port Washington, N.Y. • London

Library of Congress Catalog Card No. 73-83266
ISBN: 0-8046-9060-X

Manufactured in the United States of America

Published by
Kennikat Press, Inc.
Port Washington, N.Y./London

FOREWORD

by Douglas Bush
Gurney Professor of English Literature, Emeritus,
Harvard University

Unlike many scholars, Edward Le Comte has not confined himself to one plot of ground. He began with *Endymion in England: The Literary History of A Greek Myth* (1944). In 1955 he compiled a *Dictionary of Last Words,* a collection which exhibits the most extreme diversity of mood in the face of death and which, for the robust, may perhaps be classified as a bedside book. Two years later came *The Long Road Back: The Story of My Encounter with Polio,* a document which adds a dimension to the author's continued activity. In 1960 and 1969 he produced two novels, *He and She* and *The Man Who Was Afraid.* Between these he wrote two popular but scholarly biographies, *Grace to a Witty Sinner: A Life of Donne* (1965) and *The Notorious Lady Essex* (1969), the story of a lady, or at least a woman, who, however lacking in grace and wit, was decidedly successful as a sinner.

But Professor Le Comte's main interest has been manifest in Miltonic books and articles. The year 1961 yielded a widely used paperback edition of *Paradise Lost, Samson Agonistes,* and *Lycidas,* and *A Milton Dictionary,* a handy compendium packed with information on a broad range of topics large and small. In *Yet Once More: Verbal and Psychological Pattern in Milton* (1953) he had assembled and discussed a multitude of phrases which show Milton echoing himself in a wide variety of ways and contexts over long spaces of time—echoes which bear out the Horatian line he adapted in Geneva in 1639 for Count Cerdogni's album:

Coelum non animum muto dum trans mare curro ["My sky I change but not my mind when I cross the sea"].

A similar invincible consistency of personality and outlook is the theme of the first and longest study in the present volume, "Milton versus Time." As we should expect, Milton had his own view and experience of the great Renaissance threat of all-conquering Time, not in the pagan amorist's sense of *carpe diem* but in the Christian sense of "the night cometh when no man can work." However, the man, the poet, the tireless pamphleteer, who lived so intensely through so many public and private frustrations and vicissitudes, could not even in his early years maintain a serene assurance of personal fulfillment. Professor Le Comte, following Milton's inner and outer life from his boyhood to the end of his career, records and interprets the variations that could appear within the frame of Christian belief and feeling—in the author's words, "Milton's recurring attitudes towards time, the mortal enemy, which he seeks to arrest, or to make the most of, or to minimize, or to triumph over."

The second piece, "*Areopagitica* as a Scenario for *Paradise Lost,*" starts from some familiar parallels and spreads out into an elaborate assemblage from the tract of ideas, phrases, images, and allusions (notably to St. Paul) which can be related to the epic. Miltonic specialists may be surprised by the amount of evidence acutely observed and commented upon. Whether or not it might be subject to some discount, it illustrates the continuing vitality of Milton's characteristic modes of thought, feeling, and expression in his dealings with such themes as temptation and resistance, the divine gift of the searching mind, the strength of reason and truth, and so on. The shorter and lighter but not less learned discussion of "The Satirist and Wit" is a vigorous and racy reminder of a strain in Milton which the popular and sometimes the scholarly tradition have tended to forget.

Altogether, Professor Le Comte, experienced as he is in addressing general readers, assumes that scholarly critical studies, however weightily documented, need not be dry and austere, and he writes with zest as well as conviction.

PREFACE

This my third book on Milton pursues, as did my first, aspects of his remarkable consistency. That 1953 book, *Yet Once More: Verbal and Psychological Pattern in Milton* (reprinted AMS Press, 1969), found him repeating hundreds of phrases throughout his works, in verse and prose, in English and in Latin. I used as a motto "A mind not to be changed by place or time" (*Paradise Lost* 1:253). Now, yet once more, I echo that, for a title covering studies of (1) Milton's recurring attitudes towards time, the mortal enemy, which he seeks to arrest, or to make the most of, or to minimize, or to triumph over; (2) the strange ways in which *Areopagitica* anticipates *Paradise Lost;* (3) Milton's steady vein of satire. If I may appropriate words from a lecture of B. Rajan's published in 1973, the sum "makes evident the unifying energy of the creative mind at work and the persistence over many years of that mind's basic patterns."

The first two essays are new and have not been published before in any form. The second was written for *Achievements of the Left Hand: Essays on the Prose of John Milton,* edited by Michael Lieb and John T. Shawcross, a volume that has yet to appear. In the third essay I have made some changes since its publication in *Th'Upright Heart and Pure: Essays on John Milton Commemorating the Tercentenary of the Publication of "Paradise Lost,"* edited by Amadeus P. Fiore,

Pittsburgh, Duquesne University Press, 1967, to which press I am grateful for permission to use this material again.

Edward Le Comte

State University of New York at Albany

CONTENTS

MILTON *versus* TIME

I

"Shakespeare lived in a world of time, Milton in a universe of space."[1] This has an obviousness as regards *Paradise Lost,* which inspired the remark, but it applies to little else of Milton. Even in *Paradise Lost* one ends up with the concept of space-time, as befits an astronomical poem. The Ptolemaic clocks are spinning, sphere within sphere. The Creation is recounted, day by day, and the unfallen couple, who enjoy perpetual spring and perpetual youth, and for whom time is music, are given an alternation of night and day, a "grateful vicissitude"[2] also found in Heaven. Good gardeners, Adam and Eve keep track of the waking hours; they know when to prune and when to eat. If the last two books of the epic are a letdown,[3] they should be, presenting as they do the Fall into history (linear time versus circular time). The sun goes down now on seasons and biological change and death; there was time before, but not like this.

It can be shown that Milton, the man and the artist, was obsessed with time (as were other men of his century[4]). His poems were the bulwarks against it. When he was young he feared he was not ready. When he was older he pretended to be younger. He worried if he would have enough time, "long choosing and beginning late."[5]

"Milton, though brilliant, was retarded." This paradoxical statement comes from, not one of the eccentric critics, an Empson or a Mutschmann, but from James Holly Hanford,[6] the late dean of American Miltonists, a group not given to iconoclasm. How could Milton—or, indeed, anyone—be brilliant *and* retarded? Milton thought he was, which is a truth that has to be respected, even if posterity declares him wrong and his standards too high. "I am something suspicious of myself," he wrote a friend in the 1630s, "and do take notice of a certain belatedness in me."[7]

There is no trustworthy evidence that the child was precocious. He indicates he began speaking "imperfect words" at two:[8] nothing advanced there. Aubrey heard he was a poet at ten, but this sounds like an afterthought from the proud widow as they gazed together at the painting now in the Morgan Library. Mrs. Elizabeth Milton was not notably accurate about dates: she also said her husband entered Cambridge at thirteen. Milton's friend Charles Diodati entered Oxford at thirteen, but Milton was years tardier. If he had childhood productions of which he could be proud, it would be like him to publish them, as he published his two translations of the Psalms "done . . . at fifteen" and his English segment of Prolusio VI and an unfinished poem, "The Passion." After some initial shyness in connection with the publication of the Ludlow Castle masque, he became one who ceased to hesitate to confide his whole poetical record, good and less good, to the fit readers, however few. What he omitted in 1645 he added in 1673.

If "childhood shows the man,"[9] we see it in the serious, intent eyes of that portrait at ten[10] of one who was so obviously the delicate darling of his rich, elderly parents. But twelve marked a new stage of gravity, though not of precocity. It was then, in all probability, that he left the sheltered home, the private tutoring, to be a day pupil at St. Paul's School. That was the age of entry for the ideal academy sketched in *Of Education*. It was the time when Milton began applying himself extra hard. "My father destined me from a child for the pursuits of polite learning, which I prosecuted with such eagerness, that after I was twelve years old, I rarely retired to bed from my lucubrations till midnight."[11] Aubrey mentions 1 A.M. even, adding, "His father ordered the maid to sit up for him" as he pored over his books by candlelight. School started at 7. When did the boy sleep? He had as inspiration the school prayer for Monday afternoon: "Our Lord and Master, Sweetest Jesus, who, while yet a boy of twelve years, disputed in such manner among those doctors in the temple at Jerusalem that all were amazed at Thy most excellent wisdom. . . ."[12] Was he providing a self-portrait when he had the Savior declare, "When I was yet a child, no childish play/ To me was pleasing; all my mind was set/ Serious to learn and know, and thence to do/ What might be public good"?[13] If we never think of Dr. Johnson, say, as young, we never think of Milton as a childish child. What drove him to such lengths, and what did he pay in strain, not only eyestrain? If one part of *Paradise Regained* is personally pertinent, so is another—to wit, the Tempter's taunt that the grown man, in his thirties, is backward in view of such examples as Alexander the Great and "young Scipio" and "young Pompey": "Thy years are ripe, and over-ripe."[14]

When Milton, at thirty-seven, and again at sixty-four, was editing his poems for publication, he gave dates for some[15] of them that were too early. Looking back, he thought he must have written his Latin elegy on Gostlin the Cambridge vice-chancellor "Anno aetatis 16." This could mean "in his sixteenth year"—that is, when he was fifteen. But unlike some of his classmates he was not yet at college at that age, and from his other usage it appears he meant he was sixteen. In fact he was almost eighteen when Gostlin died on 21 October 1626. Did Milton think so little of the poem that he concluded it must have been a particularly early effusion? Or was the wish to be—and to be recognized as—a prodigy the father to the mistaken date?

In 1673 the poet added "On the Death of a Fair Infant" and gave the date of composition as "Anno aetatis 17." Here he was failing to recollect when his own niece, the "fair infant," died. She was buried 22 January 1628, when Milton was nineteen. After a lapse of forty-five years anyone is entitled to get a date wrong, but the bias is clear. The same individual, perhaps not incidentally, was poor on dates much closer and relatives much closer. We have the entries in the flyleaf of his Bible as evidence. He gave the date of his own birth with great exactitude, even to the half hour, but made no entry for his (older) sister Anne (the mother of that bygone two-year-old infant), and was tantalizing in regard to his younger brother: "Christofer Milton was born on Friday about a month before Christmass at 5 in the morning 1615." So what day was it? 17 November? 24 November? 1 December? And what is the meaning of resorting to "about" in recording the day of Mary Milton's, the first wife's, death (in childbirth)? Are some dates too painful for accuracy?

Several of Milton's letters are misdated as printed.[16] In the *Second Defence* he gets confused in chronology with reference to his Italian journey. He says he met Lucas Holste, the Vatican librarian, on his first visit to Rome, but evidently they became acquainted on Milton's second visit, as shown by Milton's own letter to Holste from Florence in the spring of 1639.[17] Also he states he returned to England at the time of the Second Bishops' War.[18] That would be in the late summer of 1640. In fact he returned a year earlier. Even the passage of fifteen years can hardly explain such large forgetfulness of an epoch both in his personal history and in that of his country. This is the scholar who remembered a thousand authors, commencing with Homer, "whose two poems he could almost repeat without book."[19]

It is a peculiar fact, hitherto unremarked on, that as regards the finest poems in his collected edition the author never says how old he was when he wrote them. The 1673 volume, like the 1645, is headed with the great ode "On the Morning of Christ's Nativity," with the note "Compos'd 1629." But the contemporary reader was nowhere provided with Milton's birthdate[20] and so did not know that this poem marked the poet's coming of age, a break with those juvenilia later deprecated as "some trifles which I . . . composed at under twenty or thereabout."[21] "This is the month" —yes indeed, it was the month of the author's twenty-first birthday. But for all the reader knew, especially the 1645 reader—before Milton became fully notorious for his controversial prose—the writer of this piece could have been fifty, or eighteen. (He looks old in the wretched frontispiece perpetrated by William Marshall, allegedly of him at twenty-one. "The face is that of a sour old fellow with a double chin and pockets under his eyes, looking exceedingly silly and trying to hide what might be a withered arm."[22]) Next came the two psalms "at fifteen"; then in 1673 the misdated "Fair Infant." According to the errata sheet of 1673, next in order was—"Anno aetatis 19"—"At a Vatican Exercise in the College." What is striking about the presentation of these two, Milton's earliest original English poems, is that the "Anno aetatis" comes first, even before the title; the apology precedes the poem. On the other hand "L'Allegro" and "Il Penseroso" have no date. Neither does "Arcades." The headnote to "Lycidas" tells only when its subject drowned. The masque now known as *Comus* has the year of first performance. Milton's age does not enter—does not need to enter—into the picture with his best work. But he prefixed it to eight of his Latin poems, while leaving undated the best—"Ad Patrem," "Mansus," and "Epitaphium Damonis."

Much about Milton's seven-year stay at Cambridge was defensive. For the first time he was living away from home, no doting parents to support his ego. Scores of his fellow students at Christ's College were younger than he.[23] Did this mean they were more precocious, or simply more puerile? Some wanted merely to "fly . . . from the government of their parents to the license of a university," not "seriously to study."[24]

At the end of his freshman year a quarrel with his tutor came to a head. Milton was suspended. Back he went to the parental home. He elaborately shrugged his shoulders in telling Diodati about it in forty-five elegiac couplets. "I don't care about returning to reedy Cam, . . . a place badly suited to the votaries of Phoebus."[25] There were ample compensations in and around London. Still, at the end, and rather lamely, he admits he is returning to the scholastic noise, the disputations.

Often, when he faced an audience there, he found hostility. Of less than average height, of delicate appearance (confirmed in another portrait with which his coming of age was celebrated), of "a certain niceness of nature, an honest haughtiness, and self-esteem of what I was or what I might be,"[26] he was nicknamed "The Lady of Christ's," as Virgil had been Parthenias, "Miss Virginity."

Sometimes he responded with scorn. "But O with what difficulty would even Heraclitus himself, if he were alive, restrain his laughter, if by chance, the gods being willing, he could perceive these little speakers here."[27] He had a particular distaste for amateur acting by the preministerial students, "writhing and unboning their clergy limbs to all the antic and dishonest gestures of Trinculos, buffoons, and bawds."[28] (So much for *The Tempest!*) In his prolusion of July 1628 he tried both scorn and imitation. After alluding to his sobriquet, "Lady," he asked, "Why do I seem to those fellows insufficiently masculine? . . . Would they could as easily lay aside their asshood as I whatever belongs to womanhood."[29] But he had already yielded to "a certain excessive desire to please,"[30] excused himself for going contrary to his usual modesty, and, playful as the elephant's "lithe proboscis" in *Paradise Lost,* labored at length to be a jolly good vulgar fellow, obscene jests and all.

Even Diodati wrote him (in Greek), "Why persist in poring over books and papers all day and all night without excuse? Live, laugh, make the most of Youth and the hours as they pass; and stop studying the activities and recreations and indolences of the sages of old, wearing yourself out in the process."

But Diodati was ahead of him, and others were ahead of him, in one way or another. Diodati achieved his Oxford

M.A. in 1628. Milton, a few months older, had four years to go for his. At the age when the one St. Paul's boy was paraphrasing Psalms 114 and 136, the other had burst into print with a Latin poem (1624).[31] In the summer of 1630 one Edward King was made a Fellow of Christ's, which Milton was never to be. The appointment was sheer politics, by order of Charles I. King was eighteen, newly B.A., one class behind Milton and three years younger. Despite his dislike of the curriculum (his assignments, he said, caused him to envy Hercules his of cleaning out the Augean stables[32]), Milton came out officially fourth among the 259 B.A.'s, university-wide, in 1629. The first three were never to be heard from. King's only enduring name is Lycidas. Diodati—"Damon"—also died young.

Milton had his own "inward prompting,"[33] his own irrefragable ideas of what "making the most of Youth" meant, and he himself proclaimed, "But headlong joy is ever on the wing."[34] His time-consciousness can be traced in poem after youthful poem.

II

His "Psalm of Life"— "Let us, then, be up and doing"—starts with Latin admonitions, evidently written as school exercises, to get up early. The boy not only stayed up late studying, but believed—was taught to believe—in rising with the sun, to make the most of daylight. The Carmina Elegiaca ("Surge, age, surge") begins and ends with the call, "Get up, come on, get up! Now it's time to shake off slumbers. It's daybreak. Leave the props of your cozy bed." Sluggards suffer from bad dreams—and bad health. He copied for a prose essay (on the reverse of the same sheet) a saw from Lily's *Latin Grammar* translated as, "To arise betime in the morning, is the most holsome thing in the worlde." You might even die before your time if you lay in bed: such is the message of eight Asclepiads warning a king or governor against oversleeping. The prose says of *somnolentia:* "It blunts and dulls keen talent, and greatly injures memory. Can anything be baser than to snore far into the day, and to consecrate, as it were, the chief part of your life to death?"[35] Everything in the three compositions found with the Commonplace Book is commonplace (including the stock diction,[36] available in phrasebooks) and expresses contemporary attitudes, partly moral, partly hygienic, partly practical in a world without even gaslight. "Day . . . alone is adapted to the transaction of business."[37] Nicholas Breton in his *Fantastics* (1626) states, incredibly, under "Two of the Clock" (A.M.): "The earnest scholar will be now at his book" (having gone to bed before eight, presumably, and of course something depends on what season it is). Of three hours later Breton remarks: "It is now five of the clock, and the sun is going apace upon his journey; and fie sluggards who would be asleep."[38] "On Time," second line, reads, "Call on the lazy leaden-stepping hours," but what may have been an earlier draft has "lazy leaden-sleeping hours."[39] Milton's first college prolusion attacks sleep: "When we set out to sleep, we tacitly confess ourselves in truth cowardly and wretched creatures, who are not able to take care of these weak little bodies for a short time without repose. And surely what else is sleep but the image and likeness of death?"[40]

Il Penseroso often stays up all night. L'Allegro is never caught sleeping. He does not miss even the lark before "the dappled dawn doth rise" (44). But as for cruder folk, "Then lies him down the lubber fiend,/And stretched out all the chimney's length,/Basks at the fire his hairy strength" (110). This is Robin Goodfellow, a special case, but the cottagers sleep also while L'Allegro goes to the theater. Milton knows who "the meaner sort"[41] are that take siestas. "The peasant snores under a hedge."[42] Milton is different. "I never lay down on my back under the sun at mid-day like a seven-year ox-driver."[43] The first thing Adam and Eve do after their Fall is to lie down—in the afternoon (sloth is one of the deadly sins)—and after carnal grapplings (newly lascivious) they are oppressed by the bad dreams of "grosser sleep."[44] The Lord finds them skulking in the woods. Samson is never so fallen as to yield to Dalila's temptation of sloth. Milton wrote in a 1654 letter, "An idle ease has never had charms for me."[45] From "Lycidas" on, the clergy were indicted for exhibiting, in addition to big-bellied greed, the two interrelated weaknesses of "ignorance and sloth":[46] they ought "to study harder" and produce something more than a sermon "huddled up at the odd hours of a whole lazy week."[47] Priests are "the most prodigal misspenders of time."[48] Of three speeches at "the great consult" in Pandaemonium only the second, Belial's, receives the poet's criticism, because it "counseled ignoble ease, and peaceful sloth,/Not peace."[49] After the Fall Adam takes the supposed curse of work in stride: "Idleness had been worse."[50]

It is inferiors who are caught sleeping by their superiors. Lucifer at the commencement of the conspiracy in Heaven bestirs "his next subordinate" with "Sleep'st thou?"[51] He asks the same question of the bad pope in "In Quintum Novembris," "Dormis?" and calls him lazy, "piger" (92,97). And who can forget the withering sarcasm the same Prince of Darkness hurls at his prostrate legions, the speech ending, "Awake, arise, or be forever fallen!" Their ashamed reaction reflects the norm:

> They heard, and were abashed, and up they sprung
> Upon the wing, as when men wont to watch
> On duty, sleeping found by whom they dread,
> Rouse and bestir themselves ere well awake.[52]

"The virtue of dutiful hard work for its own sake," even to fiendish activity, "pervades Milton. . . . The characteristic moral absolutism insists on the one ethos, the Protestant sanctification of labour, everywhere, from Paradise to Hell."[53]

Such was his upbringing—for example, the Cambridge students were herded into chapel at 5 A.M., without breakfast. It remained his creed and his practice, right up to the composition of *Paradise Lost*. "He, waking early (as is the use of temperate men), had commonly a good stock of verses against his amanuensis came; which if it happened to be later than ordinary, he would complain, saying *he wanted to be milked.*" This is the anonymous biographer; Aubrey heard the hour was 4 A.M. When the poet was twenty-five he was similarly moved—to put Psalm 114 into Greek heroic verse. "I did so with no deliberate intention certainly, but acted upon some sudden impulse. I wrote it before daybreak, while I was still practically in bed."[54] His self-description at thirty-three is: "Up and stirring, in winter often ere the sound of any bell awake men to labor, or to devotion; in summer as oft with the bird that first rouses, or not much tardier."[55] The saw from Lily about rising betimes is repeated in Milton's own improvement on that *Grammar*.[56] His earliest Latin verses about shaking off troubled sleep foreshadow Adam's aubade to Eve, on arousing her from *her* troubled sleep (devil-inspired), "Awake, the morning shines, and the fresh field/Calls us; we lose the prime."[57]

III

The earliest English poem, the "Fair Infant," sets the lifelong pattern of starting with mortality and ending with immortality. The opening lines, the first bombastically alliterative, the second tenderer, are "O fairest flower, no sooner blown but blasted,/Soft silken primrose fading timelessly!" ("blown" meaning "in bloom" and "timelessly" "unseasonably"). Todd[58] noted a debt to a quatrain in the Shakespearean collection *The Passionate Pilgrim,* which has, among other resemblances, "alack too timely shaded," but Milton's is the first recorded use of the adverb "timelessly"—as befits the time specialist that he was. Seventy-odd lines later he ends, "That till the world's last end shall make thy name to live." It little matters who this is, because fundamentally it is Milton.

This is one of the two ways to defeat death—by fame (the first resolution in "Lycidas"). Samuel Daniel copiously expressed a commonplace:

> Short-breathed mortality would yet extend
> That span of life so far forth as it may,
> And rob her fate, seek to beguile her end

Of some few ling'ring days of after-stay,
That all this little all might not descend
Into the dark a universal prey;
And give our labors yet this poor delight,
That when our days do end they are not done;
And though we die, we shall not perish quite,
But live two lives, where other have but one.[59]

Shakespeare's monument is his works, as Ben Jonson anticipated Milton in declaring. But of course Milton cannot promise fame, on the basis of their own accomplishments, to most of those he writes about, and if Henry Lawes the composer has it, the implication clearly is that Milton has greatly assisted by writing the words to which some of that music was set. Manso, Marquis of Villa, will be known because of his friendship with Tasso and Marini.

More substantial and more usual is the Christian promise of Heaven,[60] as expressed at the end of "Lycidas," or of "On Time": "Attired with stars, we shall forever sit,/ Triumphing over Death and Chance, and thee, O Time!" (The song will get better. "O may we soon again renew that song,/And keep in tune with Heaven, till God ere long/To his celestial consort us unite,/To live with him, and sing in endless morn of light." "Ad Patrem" makes a similar promise.[61]) This is what the virtuous of *Comus* have to look forward to, and in the Latin memorials, two bishops and Charles Diodati. So too, "Far within the bosom bright/Of blazing Majesty and Light" sits Jane Savage, the Marchioness of Winchester, "there clad in radiant sheen,/No marchioness but now a queen." This is the tribute of a poet who accepts hierarchy. When old Hobson the wagoner passes on, he receives only puns. The university beadle, a minor functionary, is also treated lightly.[62]

It is notable that most of the poems are occasional. "Lycidas" might never have been written if it had not been requested to help fill a memorial volume. "Arcades" and *Comus* were commissioned. Milton wrote Elegy 6 because Diodati had sent him verses. In lines 3-4 he complained,

"But why does your muse entice mine forth, not allowing her to pursue the obscurity she likes?"

Witness to his slow-measured pace with regard to that first way of opposing death is the sonnet:

How soon hath Time, the subtle thief of youth,
  Stolen on his wing my three-and-twentieth year!
  My hasting days fly on with full career,
  But my late spring no bud or blossom shew'th.
Perhaps my semblance might deceive the truth
  That I to manhood am arrived so near,
  And inward ripeness doth much less appear,
  That some more timely-happy spirits endu'th.
Yet be it less or more, or soon or slow,
  It shall be still in strictest measure even
  To that same lot, however mean or high,
Toward which Time leads me, and the will of Heaven;
  All is, if I have grace to use it so,
  As ever in my great Task-Master's eye.

What birthday does this commemorate? The heading found in many editions, "On Being Arrived at Twenty-three Years of Age," has no authority, dates from the eighteenth century. Judging by the author's Latin practice, he means by "my three-and-twentieth year" "the year in which I was twenty-three," and thus wrote his "Petrarchian stanza" (as he called it) on or soon after his twenty-fourth birthday, 9 December 1632. The context of the Letter to a Friend in which the sonnet is quoted, with its obvious references to post-Cambridge retirement, forms part of W. R. Parker's convincing argument for this date.[63] Milton was simply not a mathematician. He said of the Marchioness of Winchester, "Summer three times eight save one/She had told; alas, too soon"—which is not accurate: she had lived through twenty-four summers, although she was still twenty-three when she died. The *History of Britain* states that Turgarus expired "in the 115th year" of his age, but the Latin source says that that monk had completed a span of 115 years. The author's being twenty-four when he wrote his sonnet gives it one more year of urgency (and maturity of style) and thoroughly fits the pattern we have been tracing—of not minding being taken for younger but worrying about being older.

Of course the *tempus fugit* theme is commonplace. One could quote for line 3 that great repository of commonplaces, Seneca, the chorus in *Hippolytus,* or *Phaedra* 1141: "Volat ambiguis/Mobilis alis hora." Time has often been winged, an attribute that *De Doctrina Christiana* explains angels have in sign of swiftness.[64] Time has been a sneak-thief before. Chaucer's translation of *The Romance of the Rose* has "Tyme . . . steleth from us so prively." The exhortation to do something about it is even plainer in the Introduction to "The Man of Law's Tale":

> Lordynges, the tyme wasteth nyght and day,
> And steleth from us, what pryvely slepynge,
> And what thurgh necligence in oure wakynge.[65]

By play on the double meaning of "steal," Time is a thief in *The Comedy of Errors* IV.ii.58:

> Time is a very bankrupt, and owes more than he's worth to season.
> Nay, he's a thief too. Have you not heard men say
> That Time comes stealing on by night and day?

A seventeenth-century poetaster[66] liked Milton's conceit, such as it is, so much that he copied it: "Thercutus, when bald Time upon his wing/Had stoln his fiftieth year . . ." Here is a reminder of another commonplace, that Time (the Greek *Kairos*), like Opportunity (*Paradise Regained* 3:173), has a forelock in front, which must be grasped at once before he passes, for he is bald in back.

This leads to the question of who the "timely-happy spirits" are. Is one Spenser, the great influence on Milton at this period? Two lines in the *Amoretti* read: "Tell her the joyous time will not be staid/Unless she doe him by the forelock take."[67] Is one Sir Philip Sidney, mortally wounded at the head of his troops at Zutphen at thirty-one (mourned by Spenser in *Astrophel*), who in his twenty-third sonnet spoke of his creative "spring"?[68] Would he have had Shakespeare in mind, whose Second Folio had just come out with Milton's anonymous eight couplets of tribute in it, that Shakespeare who in his sonnets envied a rival poet, "Desiring this man's art and that man's scope" (29)? Milton in his turn envied Shakespeare his ease of composition:

> For whilst to the shame of slow-endeavoring art
> Thy easy numbers flow . . .
>
> . . . sweetest Shakespeare, Fancy's child,
> Warble his native wood-notes wild.[69]

It is more likely that "timely-happy" refers to current—and precocious—competition. "Endueth"—which means *invests*—is in the present. The first thought here would be the friendly rival, Charles Diodati, who had gone to Geneva to study divinity. (Milton was still expected to enter the ministry.) Hanford[70] conjectured, "Was there not bound to be a slight admixture of jealousy in Milton's relationship with this exuberant youth who apparently arrived at his goals with so little effort?"

Two other names get proposed. 1632 was a year of increasing glory for young Thomas Randolph of Trinity College, Cambridge, who had had two comedies published in 1630. In March he turned out by special request *The Jealous Lovers,* performed on the occasion of a visit to the university by King Charles and Queen Henrietta Maria, while Milton was still in residence. Shortly afterwards the new comedy was issued by the university press. Randolph, three years senior, had a dizzying reputation. "Probably before he had completed his four-and-twentieth year [1629], the poetical issue of his brain had been pronounced divine, comparable to Minerva, the issue of the brain of Jove, and before the end of his short life [like Marlowe he died at twenty-nine] he had come to be regarded if not as the equal of Ben Jonson, at least as one who would be no unworthy successor to him."[71] In his nondramatic poetry Randolph was mainly a pastoralist, but like Milton he produced light verses on Hobson's death and a poem much lighter than Milton's, in fact lewd, on Time, to whom he duly assigned "wings." Indeed both start out with the epithet "envious Time."[72] Sir Henry Wotton, the provost of Eton, owned in 1638 a copy of *Comus* bound with "the late R's Poems, printed at Oxford"—evidently Randolph's. *Comus* may have been a reply to the hedonism of Randolph's plays.[73]

Another poet who also happened to use what looms as a stock expression, "envious Time," in his first volume[74] is a strong candidate for having been on Milton's mind at this juncture. "My late spring no bud or blossom shew'th" looks like a topical allusion to *Poetical Blossoms* by Abraham Cowley, the boy wonder of Westminster School, where, as Randolph had been, he was King's Scholar. This slender volume was registered for publication 24 October 1632; the volume is dated 1633, but there is no need to conjecture Milton's perusing the manuscript, for publishers often anticipated the coming year to make their wares look as new as possible.[75] The connection is confirmed by the opening couplet of the boy's verses to his headmaster: "My childish Muse is in her spring, and yet / Can only show some budding of her wit."[76] In 1632 Cowley became fourteen, but the frontispiece mistakenly labeled him thirteen. Of the two tragical narratives that make up the bulk of *Poetical Blossoms,* "Pyramus and Thisbe" was written at the age "of ten years," "Constantia and Philetus" when "two years older."

Whatever Milton's later and admitted admiration for Cowley's mature work,[77] Cowley's early exercises are persistently trivial, convention-bound love poems without even the pricklings of adolescence to urge them on, and Milton needed not have brooded over *The Jealous Lovers* either, which is Randolph's worst play. But some sort of brooding he did. In transmitting the sonnet to his unidentified friend, he said, "I am the bolder to send you some of my nightward thoughts some while since, because they come in not altogether unfitly, made up in a Petrarchian stanza" (*Works,*

XII, 325). "Nightward thoughts?" Referring to the time of composition? Or to the gloom that he is writing his way out of, with the initial consciousness that "The night cometh, when no man can work" (John 9:4)?—a passage he referred to in the last sentence of his letter.

Others had bid for and received fame. Milton was waiting.[78] His name was attached to no publication. His "An Epitaph on the admirable Dramatic Poet, W. Shakespeare" was in the 1632 Folio, but anonymously. Only gradually did he reveal his authorship. It was reprinted with Shakespeare's *Poems* in 1640, with his initials. Then it became part of his 1645 collection, but with the apology of a date: 1630. He knew it was nothing to boast of. His best poem to date was the Nativity Ode, unless he had written "L'Allegro" and "Il Penseroso."

Like other mortals he would have liked Time to have a stop in his "full career." Just before going abroad in 1638 he wrote on the back of a letter from Lawes, "Fix here ye overdated spheres / That wing the restless foot of time."[79] "Overdated" means "out of date": the new astronomy had damaged the old conception of a primum mobile. Not on record in the *Oxford English Dictionary* before 1641, "overdated" is a favorite word with Milton: he uses it three times in his prose.[80] Another clue comes in *Paradise Lost,* where some of the same words are used:

> *How soon hath* thy prediction, Seer blest,
> *Measured* this transient World, the race of *Time,*
> Till Time stand fixed: beyond is all abyss—
> Eternity, whose end no *eye* can reach. . . .
> Henceforth I learn that to obey is best,
> And love with fear the only God, to talk
> *As in his presence, ever* to observe
> His providence . . .[81]

Lines 5-6 offer the beginning of consolation. He looks younger than he is. In the portrait at ten he looked eight. The newly recovered picture of him at twenty or twenty-one, since

1961 in the National Portrait Gallery, London, has an adolescent bloom: one would have guessed the subject to be not more than seventeen or eighteen. In the *Second Defence* he was to remark, "Though [I am] turned of forty, there is scarcely anyone who would not think me younger by nearly ten years."[82] But the caricature that, for want of better portraiture, had to serve as frontispiece for the 1645 *Poems* did just the opposite to him. He was, naturally, irked. The bungling portraitist—the only one that it had been possible to find in time of civil war—must be made to engrave, underneath, four lines of Greek iambics that mocked his own ineptness and invited all to make a proper comparison with nature's original. "Laugh at the inimitable picture of a rotten artist."

Smart's comment on 7-8 is of doubtful validity: "He confesses that in 'inner ripeness' he feels himself lagging behind others of his own age."[83] This becomes in an essay by Hanford[84] four years later "his sense of a lack of inward ripeness." But is Milton saying that he lacks this, or is he saying that he has it but it does not *appear?* Like a good Platonist he is separating the apparent from the real. "Endueth" means to put on, like clothing. The "timely-happy spirits" have put on their early spring finery for all to see, while Milton remains, in the adjective of his letter, "obscure" ("obscurus," "Ad Patrem" 103). A metaphor of clothing had been used in the "Vacation Exercise" 17ff, both of good style and of bad. The English language is appealed to:

> But haste thee straight to do me once a pleasure,
> And from thy wardrobe bring thy chiefest treasure;
> Not those new-fangled toys, and trimming slight
> Which takes our late fantastics with delight,
> But cull those richest robes and gay'st attire,
> Which deepest spirits and choicest wits desire.
> I have some naked thoughts that rove about,
> And loudly knock to have their passage out,
> And weary of their place do only stay
> Till thou hast decked them in thy best array.

From the inside out: this poet has not been forthcoming, like the prodigies, but the race is not always to the swift, and it would be most uncharacteristic for him at any time to fail to be conscious of—or to deny—his own inner powers. As Hanford's same essay states in a different connection, "True glory, Milton implies (and the idea is one to which he clung throughout his life) comes not from the praises of men but from the well-grounded consciousness of inner worth."[85]

All is as God decides and judges: such is the final consolation. Dorian's interpretation of the last two lines seems the most plausible: "All time is, if I have grace to use it so, as eternity in God's sight."[86] Works without grace (which secondarily means poems without style) are worthless. The lesson is, as expressed in the English letter, one of "not taking thought of being late, so it give advantage to be more fit" (the apology for Hammersmith-Horton, five years of studious retreat).

It is not that Milton is uninterested in acclaim. He acknowledged in that letter "a desire of honor and repute and immortal fame seated in the breast of every true scholar, which all make haste to by the readiest ways of publishing and divulging conceived merits—as well those that shall, as those that never shall, obtain it." (In the second draft "I know" was crossed out[87] which had made it more personal. All his life he proceeded from the personal to the general.) The sonnet glances wistfully, self-consciously, at those who have received acclaim. There may also be a compensatory tincture of disdain, as was suggested above in connection with "endueth" and as emerges further by full enough quotation from the fourth *Nemean Ode* of Pindar long taken as a source for the sestet.[88] Usually it is just one sentence that is quoted: "But, whatsoever excellence Lord Destiny assigned me, well I know that the lapse of time will bring it to its appointed perfection." But the preceding lines were: "We shall yet be deemed to come forth in the light of day far stronger than our foes, while another, with envious glance, broodeth in darkness over some fruitless purpose that falleth to the ground." As the Cambridge orator had declaimed, he meant "to strive earnestly after that true reputation by long and severe toil, rather than to snatch a false reputation by a hurried and premature mode of expression."[89]

The pagans had only one world. But Milton's eye, like that of Shakespeare's poet,[90] did "glance from heaven to earth, from earth to heaven." The Christian humanist of the Renaissance worked in acute awareness of two orders—the order of nature and the order of grace above it. In that same grand oration Milton noted, "Nothing can be recounted justly among the causes of our happiness, unless in some way it takes into consideration both that eternal life and this temporal life."[91]

Before leaving, at last, this milestone—or hourglass—of a sonnet, we must pause over line 6, which—as with some other astonishing things in Milton—commentators pass over in silence. "That I to manhood am arrived so near." He is twenty-four (or twenty-three)—and he has not reached manhood? Just what age did Milton have in mind for the beginning of manhood? Is he reverting to old Roman law, *ius vetus,* the Pandects, whereby one was a minor until age twenty-five?[92] Even the church, which accepted no fledglings, took deacons at twenty-three, admitted priests at twenty-four. (Entering the ministry is the subject, or the ostensible subject, of the Letter to a Friend enclosing the sonnet composed "some while since" —the letter that offers a general apology for "my tardy moving," "a certain belatedness.") This is truly wishful slowing of the aging process.

It sends us back to the letter to Gill of 2 July 1628 in which Milton reveals that "a certain Fellow of our house who had to act as Respondent in the philosophical disputation in this Commencement chanced to entrust to my puerility the composition of the verses according to annual custom required to be written on the questions in dispute."[93] "My puerility" ("*meae Puerilitati*"), my boyhood—ordinarily this would be taken as polite, modest deprecation. But if the author did not consider he was a man at twenty-four, he may well have thought he was still a boy at nineteen-and-a-half. He could at least have said *meae adulescentiæ*. To pass to the poetical, it is doubtful if Cephalus in "Il Penseroso" 124 should be called a "boy," considering he has been in succession the husband of Procris and the lover of Aurora, "Morn" (a sexual maturity vividly set forth in Elegia V, 40-52).

Milton's posture is all the more striking because such convention as there was went the other way: preceding poets made themselves out to be older than they were, not younger. Sir Sidney Lee[94] observes of Shakespeare: "Occasional reference in the sonnets to the writer's growing age was a conventional device—traceable to Petrarch—of all sonnetteers of the day, and admits of no literal interpretation." Daniel in *Delia* (20), at twenty-nine, lamented: "My years draw on my everlasting night, . . . My days are done." Richard Barnfield is apparently suffering from senilism at twenty: "Behold my gray head, full of silver hairs,/My wrinkled skin, deep furrows in my face."[95] Drayton may not have caught up till his mid-thirties: "Whilst thus my pen strives to eternize thee,/Age rules my lines with wrinkles in my face."[96] But at thirty-one he had already achieved "withered brows."[97]

IV

Put on the defensive by his older friend who was questioning his studious post-M.A. idleness, Milton hovers over whether to suggest that sleep—contrary to his upbringing and usual steady line—is not in all cases bad. "But if you think, as you said, that too much love of learning is in fault, and that I have given up myself to dream away my years in the arms of studious retirement like Endymion with the Moon, as the tale of Latmus goes, yet consider . . ." (*Works*, XII, 323). Apparently Endymion here is not altogether the conventional symbol of idleness that he is in a letter which an older poet, Drummond of Hawthornden, addressed to a nobleman who had gone on his travels and was assured that they "have made you more happy . . . than if, like another Endymion, you had sleeped away that swift course of days in the embracements of your mistress the court."[98] It is more the Endymion of the seventh prolusion, which praised learned and abundant leisure: "This I have believed to be the prophetic sleep of Hesiod, those nocturnal trysts of Endymion with the moon, that retreat of Prometheus under the leadership of Mercury into the deepest solitudes of Mount Caucasus, where he became the wisest of gods and men."[99] Much could be lurking in the background here—the story of Numa and Egeria, the association of caves and solitude with prophecy and divine inspiration,[100] the neoplatonic doctrine of sleep. Oracles proceeded out of caves.

> Who will foretell mutations, and of men,
> Of future things and wisely will inquire,
> Before should slumber in that shady den
> That often did with prophecy inspire.[101]

The legend of Pythagoras's cave was famous: he was in fact reputed to have got his doctrines by the mouth of the Delphic priestess. Creative sleep in a cave is referred to in "Ad Patrem," 15.[102] Moreover, Endymion, inasmuch as he was a solitary, brings to mind other philosophers and religious leaders who retreated from the company of men to find wisdom, including the Jesus of *Paradise Regained* (not to mention Mohammed in his cave of meditation at Mount Hira). Of sleep or dream or solitude as a route to wisdom, Sir Francis Bacon noted, "Divine influences sometimes steal spontaneously into the understanding when at rest, and withdrawn from the senses,"[103] what might now be called "organic thinking."

All this foreshadows the prophetic Milton, visited at night by the Holy Muse, even as Il Penseroso looked to "some strange mysterious dream" (147) and "something like prophetic strain" (174).

But Milton took his time arriving. He "was not to be hurried, even by immortality."[104] He is still hesitant, writing "Lycidas" within a few weeks of his twenty-ninth birthday, although twenty-nine is by no means young for a poet.

Yet once more, O ye laurels, and once more,
Ye myrtles brown, with ivy never sere,
I come to pluck your berries harsh and crude,
And with forced fingers rude
Shatter your leaves before the mellowing year.

He has taken up the "bud or blossom" analogy where he left it five years before. "Crude" is the Latin *crudus,* unripe. "Shatter" does not have its modern sense, as so many readers, including professionals, think, but is another form of "scatter." The leaves are just the opposite of being autumnally shatterable.

It is truly cause for astonishment that this poet, in the midst of writing what is possibly the greatest poem in the English language, should be so insistent that he is not ready to write it. What "season due" (line 7) had he in mind? These five opening lines Swinburne singled out as "the most musical in all known realms of verse."[105]

Then we come to "For Lycidas is dead, dead ere his prime." Dead not *in* his prime, but *ere* his prime. Edward King was twenty-five when he went down in the Irish Sea. The *Oxford English Dictionary's* definition 8 ("now rare") of "prime" is: "The 'springtime' of human life; the time of early manhood or womanhood, from about 21 to 28 years of age." It quotes as illustration Milton's Sonnet 9, "Lady that in the prime of earliest youth / Wisely hast shunned the broad way and the green—" but that does not help, for it is not known who the "Lady" was or how old she was. Smart took it she was a little girl. Others have guessed her to be of marriageable age, even one whom Milton thought of proposing to, such as "one of Dr. Davis's daughters" or Mary Powell. Or was it the Lady of *Comus?* Christopher Bainbrigge, Fellow of Christ's, another memorialist of King, also used "prime": "aetas/ Prima," but he did not declare that King had not attained it.[106]

Other evidence in Milton gives a wide latitude, but nothing to support "ere." "Our prime youth" in *Of Educa-*

tion[107] means the school and university years. The *History of Britain* notes that Edmund, at the time of his becoming king of East Anglia, was "a youth of fourteen years only."[108] To judge by this, Cephalus, not yet a youth, is thirteen or under. But this is pressing too hard. Milton can exhibit inconsistency even within a single poem. Jesus (at about thirty) is described by Satan in Book 1 of *Paradise Regained* (67) as grown "to youth's full flower"; at the same age in Book 4 the same observer finds him past "thy youth" and into "thy manhood" (508-9). Book 2 (200) has a reference to what Scipio Africanus did "in his prime youth": he was twenty-seven when he did it. Book 4 (508-9) mentions the four stages, "Thy infancy, thy childhood, and thy youth, / Thy manhood last," but, as we have seen, this author has peculiar notions of the boundaries of boyhood and manhood, for himself and for anyone with whom he identifies, such as Lycidas. For there can be no gainsaying that, whatever else the poem is about, it is about (as Tillyard[109] said) premature death, the blind Fury that comes so suddenly and "slits the thin-spun life." And Edward King was cut off before the full development of his talents, before his full blossoming, as the slow endeavorer Milton (there was plague all around; the body-searchers were knocking on doors and calling, "Have ye any dead?") feared *he* might be. So it is not surprising—it is even right—that "ere his prime" has not been questioned, since it is strange only in connection with data outside the poem and is emotionally true.

The poet of "Lycidas" calls himself "uncouth" (186) in the Anglo-Saxon sense of "unknown," but he has done nothing to make himself known. His second English publication has at last come out, but, like the lines on Shakespeare, anonymously, "not openly acknowledged by the author." It was Lawes, wearied of "the often copying it," that brought *A Maske Presented at Ludlow Castle* "to the public view" in forty pages. The author stood by wringing his hands by way of a motto from Virgil meaning, "Alas, what have I wished on my miserable self, for my own loss, letting the south wind in on my flowers." The next year, 1638, "Lycidas" drew up the rear of the little memorial volume *Justa Edouardo King*, with the initials "J.M.," while the author was busy polishing himself further by going on his travels (at an age six years greater than he recommended in *Of Education*).[110]

Another deprecatory motto, also from an eclogue of Virgil, appears on the title-page of the 1645 *Poems:* "Baccare frontem / Cingite, ne vati noceat mala lingua futuro." "Bind my brows with foxglove, lest an evil tongue harm the bard to be."[111] The bard to be, *"vati futuro,"* "future poet"? If he is not a poet already in a volume containing *Comus*, "L'Allegro" and "Il Penseroso," "Lycidas," and the Nativity Ode, when will he be? The context is one of being spared excessive praise and is present, even to "invidia," in the explanation for including as prefatory matter to the Latin poems the laudatory "testimonia" of the poetasters Milton had encountered in Italy. It may be that this classicist was possessed of the ancients' fear of envy, an envy that, according to Cicero,[112] the young are spared.

There are other indications in the 1645 collection of a strange mixture of pride and humility. What was the public to make of being offered an incomplete poem, with the admission, "This subject, the author finding to be above the years he had when he wrote it, and nothing satisfied with what was begun, left it unfinished."[113] Is it apology—or boast — that the separate title page of the Latin *Poemata* says that "he wrote most of them ("*pleraque*") before he was twenty"? (Of one of these the classical scholar E. K. Rand[114] was to remark, "The little epic on Guy Fawkes, the work of the author's seventeenth year, shows greater poise and firmness than the little epic on the *Gnat* which Virgil wrote at sixteen.") The reader encountered all those misleading age-dates. He also found in line 115 of "Ad Patrem" a reference to "iuvenilia carmina." The same note is struck in the Latin stanzas about the twin volume (that is, divided into English and Latin) addressed to Rouse the Oxford librarian on 27 January 1647: "Book in twin parts that rejoices in a single cover, albeit doubly wreathed, and bright with graces unlaborious, which once a youthful hand brought to you, conscientious, but not yet the hand of a master poet . . ."[115] There is something of a contradiction here between the descriptives "non operosa" (what McCrea translates as "unlaborious") and "sedula" ("conscientious"), as if Milton could not decide whether to call the poems tossed-off juvenilia (his deprecatory word to his father was "lusus," which becomes "trifles" in *The Reason of Church Government*),[116] or careful, serious work. But the last stanza appeals to posterity. By the time of the ode to Rouse youth and poetry had receded, to give the word *"olim"*—"once"—a wistful tinge and recall the Virgilian tag, "Haec olim meminisse iuvabit" (*Aeneid* 1:203).

V

By then, as everybody knows, Milton was far advanced into what was to be his twenty-year period of controversial prose. In fact he had sent to Rouse at the Bodleian, at his request, eleven pamphlets (and they are still there, bound as one volume, with the author's presentation inscription). He returned from Italy in the summer of 1639 at the news of the impending civil war, and within two years exchanged "a calm and pleasing solitariness fed with cheerful and confident thoughts" for "a troubled sea of noises and hoarse disputes,"[117] beginning with his five antiprelatical tracts of 1641-42. Nothing came from the poet, from what he called his right hand, except an occasional sonnet. Not timely-happy, but timely, it looked as if he was giving up fame for notoriety.

It is interesting that he revealed the authorship of his prose as gradually as he did that of his poems. *Of Reformation, Of Prelatical Episcopacy, Animadversions upon the Remonstrant's Defence*—are nameless. The fourth pamphlet, *The Reason of Church Government,* had to have—since it is partly autobiographical—his name, and it does. But the fifth,

An Apology for Smectymnuus, reverts to anonymity. There is a consistency here, since the fifth pamphlet answers an attack on the third, which had been anonymous (as was, indeed, the attack). These arenas were rather small, and leading opponents often felt they could guess with whom they were dealing.

Next came *The Doctrine and Discipline of Divorce,* about which there was reason to be shy. It was unsigned. Milton later explained, "My name I did not publish, as not willing it should sway the reader either for me or against me."[118] But the title page of the second, expanded edition—which was on sale 2 February 1644—bore the initials J.M., which were spelled out at the end of a prefatory "To the Parliament of England" in this edition. (A preacher before Parliament called this "impudent" and the book "wicked.") *Of Education* did not even have a title page, but was the first of the pamphlets to be registered and licensed. *The Judgment of Martin Bucer, Touching Divorce* lacked any identification on the title page but, again, contained an address "To the Parliament" that was signed. That great protest *Areopagitica* flaunted Milton's name, though it protectively concealed the publisher's or printer's name. *Tetrachordon* and *Colasterion* are "By the former author, J.M."; *Tetrachordon* also bears the full name after "To the Parliament."

Thus there is a pattern of gradual acknowledgment. On publication of *The Tenure of Kings and Magistrates,* out 13 February 1649, "The Author, J.M.," any interested parties were quite likely to know who J.M. was. The Cromwellian regime, just starting, knew, and invited Milton to be their official spokesman and secretary for foreign tongues. The first major assignment was *Eikonoklastes,* also bearing his initials. With these recent initials the author seems to be saying: "Know ye not me? . . . Not to know me argues yourselves unknown" (*Paradise Lost* 4:828,830).

In "Lycidas" Milton is appalled at the possibility of an early death, before a late bloomer can bloom. Il Penseroso looked forward to a ripe old age. In "Mansus" Milton envisioned for himself a long lifetime of composing poetry before yielding, at last, "full of years,"[119] to the ashes. He was then thirty. As he advanced into his thirties, in the 1640s, and the big poem—whether an epic or a tragedy—continued, for one reason or another, not to get written, he minimized his years. This is apparent in his sonnet "To the Lady Margaret Ley" commencing, "Daughter to that good Earl, once President / Of England's Council." Milton is addressing a woman older than himself and takes a certain pleasure in mentioning that difference: "Though later born than to have known the days / Wherein your father flourished, yet by you, / Madam, methinks I see him living yet." But her father was Lord President of the Council from 1628 to 1629, when Milton was twenty. Was that not old enough "to have known the days wherein" he "flourished"?

Another peculiar—or gratuitous—reference occurs in the preface to *The Reason of Church Government*. "And if any man incline to think I undertake a task too difficult for my years, I trust through the supreme enlightening assistance far otherwise; for my years, be they few or many, what imports it?"[120] The author was thirty-three, and who was it that complained he was too young? What readers of the previously anonymous author could even begin to guess how old he was? The reader would suppose he was hearing now an apology from a stripling. Moreover, if years do not matter, why bring up the subject? Milton is not, of course, as old as the bishops he is refuting (and he will never be old enough to get through all the church fathers), but he makes himself sound younger than he is. And he reaped his reward by being called by one of his objectors "a younge novice."[121]

In the autobiographical digression in the second book he comes back to the subject of "my youth."[122] He denies that "some self-pleasing humor of vain-glory hath incited me to contest with men of high estimation, now while green years are upon my head." He declares he has been forced to write prematurely (the same complaint as with "Lycidas"): "I should not write thus out of mine own season when I have neither yet completed to my mind the full circle of my private studies."[123] So, if the times had not forced his hand, Milton would still, at thirty-three, be preparing. And he goes on to tell what he may do as a poet, without a word as to what he has done in English since leaving school. It is all promises—a national epic, perhaps, or a drama on the Greek or Biblical model, or "magnific odes and hymns."[124] What of the hymns he had already written—the Nativity "hymn" and the smaller pieces ("At a Solemn Music" is a hymn)? For almost four years more he keeps secret their existence. How can he expect but to be what he calls himself in the next pamphlet, "of small repute"?[125]

The chronological oddities in that pamphlet have drawn the attention of two recent commentators. They rightly pause, for instance, over these early words in *An Apology*.[126]

> . . . If lastly it be but justice not to defraud of due esteem the wearisome labors and studious watchings, wherein I have spent and tired out almost a whole youth, I shall not distrust to be acquitted of presumption: knowing that if heretofore all ages have received with favor and good acceptance the earliest industry of him that hath been hopeful, it were but hard measure now if the freedom of any timely spirit should be oppressed merely by the big and blunted fame of his elder adversary; and that his sufficiency must be now sentenced, not by pondering the reason he shows, but by calculating the years he brings.

So now we have, after all these years, a "timely spirit," or, as Joan Webber[127] notes, a "hopeful youth—although at thirty-four [thirty-three] he could, if he chose, consider himself middle aged." Professor Webber goes on to observe: "The Confuter called Milton a 'grim, lowring, bitter fool,' but never a youth. This is Milton's own preoccupation—on the one hand, worrying that he has not matured fast enough; and on the other, predating himself in order to assuage his fears and to create sympathy for himself with his audience. The 'elder adversary' with his 'big and blunted fame' is made a kind of

Goliath to Milton's David." "Big and blunted" does indeed suggest a club.

Further on the author counts those years that he said do not count. And he counts wrongly. He quotes from the *Toothless Satires* by his adversary Bishop Hall, composed "when he was as young as I."[128] Not true: Hall was twenty-three, ten years younger, when his book was published in 1597; he was younger even if Milton used the third and last edition, 1602, and somehow thought it the first. But then *Areopagitica* is just as misleading about Ovid, declaring him "banished in his old age for the wanton poems of his youth."[129] The Roman poet was thirty-three when *Ars Amatoria* was published: this seems to be Milton's idea of "youth," all right, but did he really mean to call forty-three, Ovid's age at banishment, "old age"? That date probably got lost in a general recollection that Ovid did attain old age in his sad exile at Tomi, seventy-five. Milton is the last person to consider forty-three old.

A youth at thirty-three (the age at which Alexander the Great died, a significant milestone in the seventh prolusion), (*Works,* XII, 278), Milton is still a youth at thirty-five, half the Psalmist's seventy. He has discovered that a sixteenth-century reformer anticipated his views on divorce: "He knew not that what his youth then reasoned without a pattern had been heard already, and well allowed from the gravity and worth of Martin Bucer."[130] The pride here, as in opposing the bishops, is that of being fully the match of one's elders in reason, like little Jesus in the temple. Not to be blasphemous (though Christ was ever a model[131]), we shall continue to call it the "little David" complex, after, in fact, the words of Milton's nephew on the bout with "the learned Salmasius" in the 1650s: "There could nowhere have been found a champion that durst lift up the pen against so formidable an adversary, had not our little English David had the courage to undertake this great French Goliath."[132] Milton's words were: "As I should be a raw recruit engaging with a veteran, there were many who dissuaded me from the undertaking, partly out of envy, lest, whatever the issue, I should gain glory from a contest with an enemy so illustrious; partly, from apprehension for me and for the cause, lest I should retire vanquished, to the heavy disgrace of both."[133]

From "timely-happy spirits" to "timely spirit": Milton has decided to become the prodigy he once envied. The contemporary reader, in no position to calculate the years of the unknown author, would scarcely conjure up from his "youth" references a man in his thirties. If of the learned sort himself, he would think of someone paralleling the biblical translator John Bois, who versified in Latin, Greek, and Hebrew before he was ten, was elected Fellow of St. John's, Cambridge at nineteen, and became Lecturer in Greek at twenty-two.[134] Or, among Continental prodigies, were the celebrated Claude de Saumaise, whose first learned book appeared when he was twenty; and Alexander More, professor of Greek at Geneva at twenty-three—an age at which Milton was still under the authority of professors. If the young Milton allowed himself few hours of sleep at night, Saumaise as a teenager went further still. He frequently stayed up with his books all night, two out of three nights, with the consequence that he became seriously ill.[135]

When he dueled in Latin with those two, Salmasius and Morus, in the 1650s, Milton subjected various aspects of their lives to hostile review, as they did his. He says nothing, perhaps knew nothing, about Salmasius as an early achiever. He quoted from Salmasius's first book, but in an edition thirty-seven years later.[136] He calls him old (at sixty-one).[137] Of Morus's first position *Defensio Secunda* merely says, "This personage, to pass over the obscurity of his early life, first made his appearance as teacher of Greek at Geneva; and though he often explained to his scholars the meaning of his own name, Morus, in Greek, he could not himself unlearn to be a fool, and a profligate."[138] Considering all the variations rung on More's name, what about *sophomoric* here? However, the *responsio* at the end of *Defensio Pro Se,* 1655, gets into the question of early flowering in the only direct verbal conflict between Milton and a self-proclaimed prodigy. (Incidentally, both were at Geneva in June 1639, the one at thirty on his way home to England, the other at twenty-three angling for his Greek professorship.) More having called Milton a suddenly sprung-up mushroom is answered, "You mistake, More, and know me not. . . . You are that mushroom, who, when only just out of your boyhood, went to Geneva, and all at once popped up professor of Greek." Milton points the contrast. "To me it always appeared best to grow slowly, and as it were, by imperceptible advances." Slow and hidden growth ("lente crescere et velut occulto aevo")[139]—Time, the subtle thief. "They also serve who only stand and wait." It was slower than ever now, with blindness. Two sonnets thirty years apart and the Letter to a Friend about belatedness meet here at this polemical exchange.[140] As for the folly of attempting something while unripe, Milton could comment both as student and teacher, and he emphatically did in *Of Education:*[141] "forcing the empty wits of children to compose themes, verses, and orations, which are the acts of ripest judgment" and "these are not matters to be wrung from poor striplings, like blood out of the nose, or the plucking of untimely fruit."

Salmasius was a shallow grammarian and Morus a libidinous fool. Their confuter, continuing at this period his *History of Britain,* was to note that King Edgar died in his thirty-second year, "before the age wherein wisdom can in others attain to any ripeness."[142] The dubious sources made Athelstane another exception: "He was thirty years old at his coming to the crown, mature in wisdom from his childhood, comely of person and behavior."[143] In 1660, making a last appeal to his backsliding countrymen before the Restoration, he asked, "Shall we never grow old enough to be wise?"[144] He has seen the folly of actions performed in the "heat of youth."[145]

Just as there were two civil wars, so there were two

phases in Milton's polemic career. From the spring of 1645 through 1648 he was not heard from in prose. He had published eleven pamphlets and had reason to be discouraged. They had received the wrong kind of attention or none at all. He was like a prolific author with a total of about five notices —all bad. The glorious *Areopagitica* was ignored, totally ignored. Scholars have combed through thousands of contemporary pamphlets without finding a single reference to it in the period of the 1640s.[146] The same applies to *Of Education,* which was possibly a private printing for circulation among friends (as "Epitaphium Damonis" had been in 1640). The big name here was Comenius, not Milton. Milton contemptuously gives him a passing dismissal without naming him. He also refused to name William Prynne, a controversialist of great contemporary fame, as would be, a little later, John Lilburne the Leveler and Marchamont Needham, the witty journalist. It was no wonder that the neglected author, with savage gratitude, answered whatever casual attack he received. He pathetically waited for a worthier opponent than the "serving-man" "dolt" he whipped in *Colasterion.* "Thus much to this nuisance. But . . . if any man equal to the matter shall think it appertains him to take in hand this controversy . . ."[147] No one did, though the *Doctrine and Discipline of Divorce* continued to raise eyebrows briefly and one Baptist she-preacher ran away with another woman's husband on the strength of it.[148] Latin would have drawn better readers;[149] he had cast pearls to swine (Sonnet 12).

So, for the greater part of four years, Milton gave up exhorting his countrymen in prose. He very likely meant to give up for good. His wife Mary returned to him from Oxford after three years of desertion, and two daughters were born. The house in the Barbican, large though it was, was crowded with pupils and refugee in-laws. There, within three months of each other, passed away Milton's father-in-law and his elderly father. The mother-in-law remained, a definite thorn intestine. Milton wrote of domestic troubles in a wistful letter of 21 April 1647 on hearing from his Tuscan friend of nine years before, Charles Dati:

A something heavier creeps in upon me, to which I am accustomed in very frequent grievings over my own lot: the sense, namely, that those whom the mere necessity of neighborhood, or something else of a useless kind, has closely conjoined with me, whether by accident or by the tie of law, *they* are the persons, though in no other respect commendable, who sit daily in my company, weary me, nay, by heaven, all but plague me to death whenever they are jointly in the humor for it, whereas those whom habits, disposition, studies, had so handsomely made my friends, are now almost all denied me, either by death or by most unjust separation of place, and are so for the most part snatched from my sight that I have to live well-nigh in a perpetual solitude.[150]

That word "sight" ("conspectu"), he did not say he was losing it, but he was, the left eye first, and his health was poor, possibly from his experiments with self-treatment. But he mentioned the 1645 *Poems*. "Yet, even in the midst of these evils, since you desire to be informed about my studies, know that we have published not a few things in our native tongue; which, were they not written in English, I would willingly send to you, my friends in Florence, to whose opinions I attach very much value. The part of the Poems which is in Latin I will send shortly, since you wish it."[151] He worked on several prose manuscripts, the beginnings of his *De Doctrina Christiana*, the short *History of Moscovia*, the first four books of the *History of Britain*, but he was struggling to get back to poetry, as witness the poor sonnet "On the Religious Memory of Mrs. Catharine Thomason" of December 1646 and the painful metrical translations in April 1648 of Psalms 80-88. Parker is the leader of the scholars who place the composition of *Samson Agonistes*, most of it, in this period.

However that may be—and this unorthodox date for *Samson Agonistes* remains very doubtful—it took a most extraordinary event to lure Milton back into the public arena: the trial and execution of King Charles I. The king was beheaded outside his palace of Whitehall on 30 January 1649, an act that forced a groan from even the most republican of the witnesses. By 13 February the bookstalls had *The Tenure of Kings and Magistrates: Proving That It Is Lawful, and Hath Been Held So Through All Ages, for Any, Who Have the Power, to Call to Account a Tyrant, or Wicked King, and After Due Conviction, to Depose, and Put Him to Death, If the Ordinary Magistrate Have Neglected, or Denied to Do It.* Exactly one month later the regicide government invited the author to join it in the capacity of translator and official defender. He did not hesitate. Here was fulfillment of sorts for a man who had long felt useless and frustrated as he turned from one self-assignment to another, uncertain of all, the "talent which is death to hide" hidden. As Parker notes, "Having been so long denied an appropriate demonstration of his usefulness, he laboured like a man possessed."[152] He first put out, without his name or initials, *Observations upon the Articles of Peace with the Irish Rebels,* of which an interesting side feature is an oblique blurb for his own *Tenure* (which had the same printer-publisher). Referring to the government's declaration in justification of itself (which Milton had already put into Latin), he told his audience, "Books also have been written to the same purpose for men to look on that will."[153] (Such transparent impersonality has its charm, as it does in the divorce tracts, and in the recommendation in *Of Education* for the Latin grammar that Milton is going to publish: "They should begin with the chief and necessary rules of some good grammar, either that now used, or any better,"[154] and had he in mind a translation of his *De Doctrina Christiana* when he spoke in *Considerations Touching the Likeliest Means to Remove Hirelings out of the Church* of helps "to make more easy the attainment of Christian religion by the meanest": "Somewhere or other, I trust, may be found some wholesome body of divinity . . . without school terms and metaphysical notions, which have obscured rather than explained our religion, and made it seem difficult without cause."[155])

Duty next called him to a rather awkward task, shooting down the ghost of King Charles as it strode the land in a bestselling book designed to whip up sympathy for him, *Eikon Basilike,* "The King's Image," *The True Portraiture of His Sacred Majesty in His Solitudes and Sufferings.* Milton started his *Eikonoklastes,* "The Image-Breaker," with apology: "To descant on the misfortunes of a person fallen from so high a dignity, who hath also paid his final debt both to nature and his faults,[156] is neither of itself a thing commendable, nor the intention of this discourse. Neither was it fond ambition, or the vanity to get a name, present or with posterity, by writing against a king; I never was so thirsty after fame, nor so destitute of other hopes and means, better and more certain to attain it."[157] Further on he alluded to bad poets who (to borrow the words of "Lycidas") "think to burst out into sudden blaze": "To bad kings, who without cause expect future glory from their actions, it happens as to bad poets, who sit and starve themselves with a delusive hope to win immortality by their bad lines."[158] Both at the beginning and end this image-breaker assails the "new device of the king's picture at his prayers,"[159] "the conceited portraiture . . . drawn out to the full measure of a masking scene, and set there to catch fools and silly gazers,"[160] the frontispiece by William Marshall, who made Charles far more attractive than he had made Milton some three years previously.

Eikonoklastes was prolix, as the book it answered was, and its author realized the futility of trying to convince "the blockish vulgar";[161] how could reason prevail against sentimentality, the irrational canonization of the martyr-king? One could only hope for fit audience, though few: "to find out . . . readers, few perhaps, but those few . . . of value and substantial worth."[162] *Eikon Basilike,* which proved impossible to suppress, went through some sixty editions in one year. *Eikonoklastes,* with all the force of officialdom behind it, had two. Milton knew what sold, as did the publisher of his 1645 *Poems* (which did not sell), who complained: "The slightest pamphlet is nowadays more vendible than the works of learnedest men." Pseudodivinity sold, as found at the end of every chapter of *Eikon Basilike,* "clapped together and quilted out of Scripture phrase, with as much ease and as little need of Christian diligence or judgment, as belongs to the compiling of any ordinary and saleable piece of English divinity that the shops value."[163] These prayers attributed to the king "perhaps may gain him after death a short, contemptible, and soon fading reward."[164]

But Milton warmed to his task and he especially warmed to his next big assignment of answering Salmasius, whose *Defensio Regia* was doing the sort of damage on the Continent that *Eikon Basilike* did at home. The *Pro Populo Anglicano Defensio* brought him international reputation, and he basked in it. He gave his eyes, but it was worth it:

> What supports me, dost thou ask?
> The conscience, friend, to have lost them overplied
> In liberty's defence, my noble task,
> Of which all Europe talks from side to side.[165]

A variant for "talks" is "rings" (which takes us back to—and makes an equation with—the praise of the man of action, Lord General Fairfax, "whose name in arms through Europe rings"). Henry Oldenburg, agent for Bremen—and many readers since—lamented the waste of genius. Milton answered, "I am far from thinking that I have spent my toil, as you seem to hint, on matters of inferior consequence."[166]

The point here is not to argue again whether he was right, but to note that he had to think he was. We are in the presence of three rationalizations:[167] (1) if the big poem is not forthcoming, it is because still more preparation is necessary; (2) besides, prose, even mud-slinging or citation-bogged prose, may also be a proper use of God's talent; (3) anyway, there is still time.

To take up 3 again, the pattern of peculiarity continues. Apropos of the ode to Rouse, Parker says of the poet, "He had recently turned thirty-eight and his youth was now behind him."[168] Who would disagree, especially as these and subsequent years weighed more heavily then than they do now? The average person was lucky not to be dead at forty. But Milton would disagree. He began his 1652 sonnet to Sir Henry Vane, "Vane, young in years, but in sage counsel old." Vane was thirty-nine. Indeed, Parker presents a contradiction of his own normal position a few pages further on when in one sentence he observes that "the Biblical Samson was about forty"[169] and quotes Milton's line about him, "in my flower of youth and strength" (line 938). Flower of youth—defined by Terence as sixteen (*Eunuchus* 318). "Flower of youth" at forty? Perhaps, if one is "ere his prime" at twenty-five and a "boy" after having had a wife and a mistress.

Shakespeare would not have agreed, having written of a man in Sonnet 2, "When forty winters shall besiege thy brow/ And dig deep trenches in thy beauty's field." The Earl of Salisbury at forty-four was described by Jonson[170] as having entered "the twilight of sere age." Milton, always the revolutionary, is ahead of his time, a modern youth cultist.

So we need not be too surprised when, at the age of forty-three, he starts the great sonnet on his blindness, "When I consider how my light is spent, / Ere half my days in this dark world and wide." He expects to live to be more than eighty-six?[171] Why not? He could use the time, slowed now by an obstacle that would have silenced an ordinary man forever. His father reached his mid-eighties. Isocrates, the "old man eloquent,"[172] was a favorite reference—who attained ninety-eight. Identification with various Old Testament figures came easily to the Puritans. In 1652 Milton became a father for the fourth time. Abraham begot Isaac at one hundred. A recent commentator,[173] going Milton one better, quotes Isaiah 65:20: "There shall be no more thence an infant of days, nor an old man that hath not filled his days; for the child shall die an hundred years old but the sinner being an hundred years old shall be accursed." Maybe that is the ultimate dream, to be a child at one hundred. In 1653 Milton put into couplets Psalm 1 about the righteous man being like a tree which "in his season knows / To yield his fruit, and his leaf shall not fall, / And what he takes in hand shall prosper all." *De Doctrina Christiana* observes that "God, at least after the fall of man, limited human life to a certain term, which in the progress of ages, from Adam to David, gradually became more and more contracted; so that whether this term be one and the same to all, or appointed differently to each individual, it is in the power of no one to prolong or exceed its limits."[174] But it is also pointed out that there are those "who accelerate death by intemperate living"[175] (which one amateur theologian had no intention of doing). A recent critic has grasped the point exactly. "Milton had to give himself time; his great poem was not yet written."[176]

The author of *Defensio Secunda,* 1654, making a statement about himself in answer to attack, is more evasive about his age than his stature. Let them call him small, if they like. He would rather not say that he is forty-five. He says he is past forty, looks about ten years younger, with eyes that do not betray that he is blind.[177] Nine years later, when, having outlived two wives, he married for the third time, he did not find it necessary to specify his age as fifty-four. The marriage allegation reads: "about 50 years." His young bride Elizabeth Minshull obligingly advanced herself a year to narrow the gap. Recently twenty-four, she answered "about 25." This is all very human, of course: many a man would say the same, indeed does, in these circumstances. It also happens to be very Miltonic. A similar vagueness on legal occasions leaves the year of his father's birth still unknown.

Defensio Secunda is the most sustained expression of rationalization 2—that the *Defensio Prima,* which nobody reads today, was its author's crowning achievement. He crows over his routed opponent. "There are not wanting . . . those who lay the guilt of his death upon me, and upon those stings of mine which were but too sharp; and which, by resisting, he caused to sink the deeper."[178] Milton is far from denying the possibility or expressing regret. "I and my concerns (though in no wise free from the ills of humanity) are under the care of the Deity."[179] Megalomania alternates with euphoria. "It is not possible for me, nor can it ever be my desire, to ascribe to myself anything greater or more glorious."[180]

But he also says he has been holding himself back, a declaration which makes sense only with reference to his poetry.

Who and whence I am, say you, is doubtful. So also was it doubtful, in ancient times, who Homer was, who Demosthenes. The truth is, I had learnt to be long silent, to be able to forbear writing, which Salmasius never could; and carried silently in my own breast what if I had chosen then, as well as now, to bring forth, I could long since have gained a name. But I was not eager for fame, who is slow of pace; indeed, if the fit opportunity had not been given me, even these things would never have seen the light; little concerned, though others were ignorant that I knew what I did. It was not the fame of everything that I was waiting for, but the opportunity. Hence, it happened, that I was known to no small number of persons, before Salmasius was known to himself.[181]

This is obviously a statement of central importance on growth and fame and time.

The postscript to the revised edition of *Defensio Prima,* 1658, still makes the Horatian claim of "a memorial which, such as it is, I see will not easily perish."[182] This was reasserted, in English, in 1660: "a written monument likely to outlive detraction."[183] But the very last words in 1658 are a promise: "I . . . consider chief how I may bear best witness—not only to my own country, to which I have paid the highest I possessed, but even to men of whatever nation, and to the cause of Christendom above all—that I am pursuing after yet greater things if my strength suffice (nay, it will if God grant), and for their sake meanwhile am taking thought, and studying to make ready."[184] *Paradise Lost* will not be lost, after all. At least one hopes he was referring to the epic, rather than *De Doctrina Christiana,* or worse yet, those 1659 publications *A Treatise of Civil Power in Ecclesiastical Causes* and *Considerations Touching the Likeliest Means to Remove Hirelings out of the Church.*

VI

Besides having in succession three young wives, the first seventeen when he was thirty-three, Milton enjoyed the company of youth. We gather it was that, not lack of sufficient income from investments, that made him a tutor to his two nephews and several other young gentlemen of his acquaintance in his thirties. He had educational theories to try out. In his forties and blind, he still takes on one pupil, Richard Jones, the son of Lady Ranelagh, and monitors his progress when he travels abroad. Later there is the son of the poet Davenant. There are young men or boys who read to him and who act as amanuenses and perhaps escort him through the streets ("A little onward lend thy guiding hand," *Samson Agonistes* 1). Indeed of this period Parker notes, "As he grew older, Milton was more and more attracted to the young, and he gathered about him a group of devoted disciples."[185] It is a familiar feeling, not exclusive to teachers, that the young will help preserve against getting old. Milton had Cyriack Skinner, the grandson of Sir Edward Coke (Sonnets 20, 21). There was Andrew Marvell the poet (in his early thirties but young enough), whom Milton recommended for assistant Latin secretary and who wrote him from Eton on 2 June 1654 that he was "exceeding glad to think that Mr. Skyner is got near you, the Happiness which I at the same Time congratulate to him and envie."[186] There was Edward Lawrence, son of the lord president of Cromwell's council, the recipient of the sociable, even mildly bibulous Sonnet 20. Richard Heath, proud to be called an "alumnus," wrote him gratefully. The Quaker Thomas Ellwood began at twenty-two as a reader in Latin, ended up fancying he had given the initial inspiration for *Paradise Regained.* There were admiring young visitors and correspondents from abroad, such as Peter Heimbach and Emeric Bigot and Henry de Brass. This is not to mention the three daughters; the two who were physically and mentally able eventually read out loud in several languages and took dictation.

Thus surrounded by the young, Milton is a perpetual

student who still at fifty speaks of himself in terms of growing maturity. The prefatory address to the Parliament in the *Considerations* (a pamphlet that confidently assumes knowledge of its author's immediately previous one) petitions with a familiar mixture of pride and humility, requesting "but this, that if I have prosperously, God so favoring me, defended the public cause of this commonwealth to foreigners, ye would not think the reason and ability whereon ye trusted once (and repent not) your whole reputation to the world, either grown less by more maturity and longer study."[187] A man at fifty may consider himself wiser than he was in his forties, but both decades would seem to be too far along in life for hinting that one was not mature ("more" inevitably suggesting there had been a youngish lack).

Paradise Lost came out when its author was fifty-eight, *Paradise Regained* and *Samson Agonistes* when he was sixty-two—in other words, dangerously late. And he realized it. The talents were nearly buried, deep in the ground. (Spenser was not granted time to finish *The Faerie Queene*.) All three of these last poems are dogged by doubt, followed by reassurance.

To take them in reverse order, it goes against the grain to think of *Samson* as pre-Restoration (as Parker would have us do) when it contains so many post-Restoration allusions. Indeed, one of Parker's arguments[188] is curiously ivory-towered, namely that because the drama sounds so personally applicable it must have been written at a time when less of it did apply—for instance, when Milton still had his eyesight and the Philistines had not triumphed in England. One recognizes the English professor holding forth that Thomas Wolfe is a bad novelist *because* he is autobiographical, in which case Walt Whitman is a bad poet, and so by the same token Milton, unless we save him by predating him. Such zeal not to commit "the autobiographical fallacy" overlooks that Milton in a number of places elsewhere is unabashedly personal. He did not mind discussing his marital preferences in public in 1642: "I . . . would choose a virgin of mean fortunes, honestly bred, before the wealthiest widow."[189] In 1671, if he had anything to hide (which is arguable), the disguise of drama was sufficient.

One suspicious feature is that Samson sounds elderly. Despite the astonishing reference to him as being in the "flower of youth" (938), despite his historically presumed forty years, "old age" keeps getting mentioned (572,700,925, 1487, and only once before, in *P.L.* 11:538). Of course it is partly his helpless blindness (1489) and partly his hopeless frame of mind and the way he keeps looking back over his past, but he seems a fit candidate for an old folks' home. He has insomnia (459,629). He anticipates the gout (571; cf. 698-700), which Milton suffered from (medically a sign of ambition[190]). He declares he will "shortly be with them that rest" (598). Manoa wants him to retire: "Better at home lie bed-rid, not only idle,/Inglorious, unemployed, with age outworn" (579). Dalila says she wants to nurse him at home. But he dies in action, his last work his greatest. "He, though blind of sight, / Despised, and thought extinguished quite, / With inward eyes illuminated, / His fiery virtue roused / From under ashes into sudden flame" (1687) went out in a blaze of glory. "Sudden flame" recalls the "sudden blaze" of "Lycidas" (74). In sum there is warrant for the title of Hanford's essay, "*Samson Agonistes* and Milton in Old Age." The latest theories are not necessarily the truest.

The personal note may first have been struck in the preface, the fear of never being able to meet one's own high standards. "Augustus Caesar also had begun his *Ajax*, but, unable to please his own judgment with what he had begun, left it unfinished" (I:331-32). It happens that the last four of these words had appeared in 1645, appended to the unfinished poem "The Passion": "The author, . . . nothing satisfied with what was begun, left it unfinished." There is even an article entitled "Is *Samson Agonistes* Unfinished?"[191]—fortunately not very convincing.

Paradise Regained, most of which Parker also dates before *Paradise Lost* (!),[192] fits into Milton's pattern of anxiety. Jesus at thirty is "obscure, unmarked, unknown" (1:24). The Tempter tries to lure him to vainglory. But, for one answer.

what is to be thought of "The people's praise . . . A miscellaneous rabble" (3:48,50)? Another point is that the user of words is superior to the military conqueror (1:222). A third answer is that even Satan is made to concede that to God "longest time . . . is short" (1:56). The Savior puts this more deliberately, after the manner of Sonnets 7 and 19: "And time there is for all things, Truth hath said" (3:183). ("Due time" is a significant recurrence: 3:181,440.) So there is no need to be unduly bothered by anyone's mentioning such world-famous prodigies as Alexander the Great and "young Scipio" Africanus. As for the Tempter's third example, "Young Pompey quelled / The Pontic king and in triumph had rode" (3:35), explanation might well be demanded, for "young Pompey" was older than Jesus—he was even older than Sir Henry Vane—at the time of the two accomplishments mentioned. He conquered Mithridates at forty, and rode in triumph in Rome at forty-five. So either the Devil is proving himself the father of lies or Milton in his sixties thinks forty-five "young." Need we choose, both being so plausible?

The British critic Frank Kermode, making an approach based on Erik Erikson's life-cycle analysis in *Young Man Luther,* finds Milton identifying with Jesus—and with Cromwell. "In his youth" Milton

> was not a consciously revolutionary figure, not opposing the Church of England and certainly not the monarchy. He probably didn't know what he wanted, except that he wanted time. Of course, if you delayed too long you might die before emerging into the great world. But Italy made him feel more secure, more mature; he was honoured, and brought honour to English civility, liberty, scholarship and religion. And so he hurried back, aged 30, to fight for the revolutionary cause, to begin his peculiar ministry. Thirty is a significant age. Milton started out at the same age as Jesus. When he wrote *Paradise Regained,* which is about perfect heroism and the exemplary hero Jesus, he chose the moment when the hero emerges from seclusion, the primary heroic crisis. Until 30 his hero prepared himself by study and devotion, accepting his mother's advice to delay. So, says Jesus, "The time prefixed I waited" [1:269]. Then he emerges, ready to meet every possible temptation, and after enduring that, he finds "all his great work

to come before him set" [2:112]. But, says Milton, he hardly knows even now what that work is. And when Milton wrote about Cromwell, who was the kind of active hero he himself might have liked to be, he made him fit the same pattern: "He grew up in the privacy of his own family, and till his age was quite mature and settled, which he also passed in private, was chiefly known for his attendance upon the purer worship, and for the integrity of his life. . . . He had nursed his great spirit in silence."

[*Works,* VIII, 213][193]

In the summer of 1667, a few weeks before *Paradise lost. A Poem Written in Ten Books* went on sale, Abraham Cowley, the prodigy, passed away at forty-nine in his country retreat in Chertsey, leaving his religious epic *Davideis* unfinished. Cowley cuts a very different figure in the Civil War from the heroic Milton. Having served abroad as a Royalist spy, he returned for the same purpose to England in 1654, was imprisoned by the Puritan government, but made his submission, and ended up being distrusted by both sides. In the preface to his 1656 *Poems* he explained how it was necessary to yield to authority.[194] Milton in his note on the verse in *Paradise Lost* is still resisting "bondage"—in this case the "modern bondage of rhyming." Cowley had a splendid funeral (burial in Westminster Abbey beside Spenser and Chaucer) and a period of popularity that the eighteenth century found incredible. Of the monotonously coupleted *Davideis* Dr. Johnson[195] observed, "Nothing can be more disgusting than a narrative spangled with conceits, and conceits are all that [the *Davideis*] supplies." "Who now reads Cowley?" asked Pope,[196] who pilfered phrases from Milton.

By now it should come as no surprise—but rather as an authenticating signature—that *Paradise Lost* also has an extraordinary age reference. First there is a description that sounds like pre-Restoration London in parliamentary turmoil:

> In other part the sceptred heralds call
> To council in the city-gates: anon
> Grey-headed men and grave, with warriors mixed,
> Assemble, and harangues are heard, but soon
> In factious opposition.
>
> [11:660]

At this juncture a man not named gives wise but rejected counsel:

> till at last
> Of middle age one rising, eminent
> In wise deport, spake much of right and wrong,
> Of justice, of religion, truth and peace,
> And judgment from above; him old and young
> Exploded, and had seized with violent hands . . .
> [664]

The Latinism "exploded" means "shouted down" or "jeered" —exactly the fate of the author of *The Ready and Easy Way to Establish a Free Commonwealth.* This middle-aged personage receives a total of twenty-one lines without being named. He prophesies, as Milton does at the end of *Paradise Lost.* He appears in a period when "what most merits fame" is "in silence hid" (699). Would Milton in his later fifties at last grant that *he* has reached middle age? If so, there is as much reason (and modesty) in identifying him with this figure as with the lone dissenting angel Abdiel. This seventeenth-century prophet found himself, if not "righteous"—right, "in a world perverse" (701). "With dangers compassed round" (7:27) he feared for his life at the "violent hands" of the sons of Belial. A regicide with his pen, he narrowly escaped being one of the exceptions in the general pardon, the Indemnity Bill. His friend Harry Vane was executed. Milton had to go into hiding, was arrested and imprisoned, and on being let go lived, according to Richardson,[197] "in perpetual terror of being assassinated, though he had escaped the talons of the law. He knew he had made himself enemies in abundance. He was so dejected he would lie awake whole nights."

To get back to the middle-aged figure in Book 11, he is identified by his end: "A cloud descending snatched him thence / Unseen amid the throng" (670). He is Enoch. And how old was he? He had (perhaps not coincidentally) as many years as there are days in the solar year, 365 (Genesis 5:23). "Of middle age"? Yes, as patriarchs went, and especially as the father of Methuselah,, who lived to be 969.

But the final fascination of Enoch is that, at 365, he did not die but was translated to "the climes of bliss" (708). He was "Exempt from death" (709).

The author of Genesis, with whom Milton identifies at the beginning of his poem, reached 120. When this "servant of the Lord died there in the land of Moab" "his eye was not dim, nor his natural force abated" (Deuteronomy 34:5,7). In the former respect he was like Milton's father, who "read without spectacles at 84." One very significant connection with the poet himself is that Moses was "slow of speech" (Exodus 4:10) until kindled by the Lord. The encyclopedic Renaissance view of the epic was that it could not be struck out in the "heat of youth" but "can only be completed late in life . . . it takes time to mature a scholar and still more time to unite scholarship with poetic skill."[198]

The invocations to *Paradise Lost* are a mixture of confidence and anxiety. Milton at once puts his readers on notice to expect a unique and superior poem. He will outfly the ancients because he has a better muse, the Holy Spirit, and a bigger and truer subject. There is none of the modesty, mock or genuine, of Cowley and such immensely successful authors as Burton and Walton (Milton is taking on "prose" rivals too, 1:16). " 'Tis not worth the reading, I yield it," Burton is still saying in his revised sixth edition of *The Anatomy of Melancholy*.[199] "The Epistle to the Reader" of *The Compleat Angler*[200] disarmingly suggests "that he that likes not the book" may perhaps like the illustrations. How far such asides are from "the most competitive of poets!"[201]

With Book 3 he faces up to his blindness and indicates it has its advantages of inner sight, insight. Also that other darkness, sleep, has become inspirational: "Nightly I visit" (32); "thou visit'st my slumbers nightly" (7:28); "my celestial patroness . . . her nightly visitation" (9:21). As Eve says, translating from the *Iliad*, "God is also in sleep, and dreams advise."[202]

But there is insecurity, too: can the flight continue? Blindness is also movingly presented as a personal handicap

(3:22ff). Physical danger looms (7:24ff). Late in the poem three reasons are given for possibly failing: being born at the wrong time and place—"an age too late, or cold / Climate" (9:44)—or, yes, being, in the late fifties, too old: "years" may "damp my intended wing / Depressed." It is a race against time and disease and death.[203] As Michael expands—or expounds—the subject:

> for the air of youth,
> Hopeful and cheerful, in thy blood will reign
> A melancholy damp of cold and dry
> To weigh thy spirits down, and last consume
> The balm of life.
>
> [11:542]

VII

"Fit audience find, though few" (7:32). Most of the time Milton realized he was destined neither for "sudden blaze" nor "broad rumor"—widespread popularity. He luxuriated in the fame his *Pro Populo Anglicano Defensio* brought him. He would not have minded if his English pamphlets had won a wider credit. But the virtuous and the knowing are in the minority; and the best which could be hoped was that the truth he was offering would "find out her own readers: few perhaps, but those few such of value and substantial worth as truth and wisdom, not respecting numbers and big names, have been ever wont in all ages to be contented with."[204] And in times of greatest depression, when even the wisest seemed not to be listening, there was the "perfect witness of all-judging Jove" to appeal to: "As he pronounces lastly on each deed, / Of so much fame in Heaven expect thy meed" ("Lycidas" 83). "Jove" was the Christian taskmaster in the similar consolation of Sonnet 7, and would be again. The man of the Renaissance felt no impropriety in using a classical name for Christian deity: so the Greek of Eve's "God is . . . in sleep" has the genitive of "Zeus" (which, however, in the oblique cases—*Dios*—sounds like "Deus"). Which leads into David Daiches's comment on "Lycidas" 83-4: "The pat aphoristic nature of that final couplet could not possibly be a solution to such a complex poem as *Lycidas*. There is almost a note of irony in the copy-book lesson. It is a deliberately false climax."[205]

There was indeed an aphorism, but none of the commentators quote it. But Ben Jonson quoted it, in Greek, as the title or heading of his epitaph on Katherine, Lady Ogle.[206] It occurs in the standard Greek lexicon of the time, *Stephani Thesaurus,* as a "Proverbium apud Zenobium": "Zeus, from above, in the fullness of time, looks at the records." Jonson's poem begins, " 'Tis a record in Heaven."

God was Milton's witness, his ideal reader. God was also increasingly his subject, and God or Heaven was his refuge. In writing his transcendental poetry Milton was fleeing "envious time." Such an aperçu was, in passing, A.S.P. Woodhouse's[207] when he linked "On Time" with Sonnet 7. "There Milton has stayed by an act of Christian self-dedication the disquieting thought of Time, which has stolen youth without bringing assured maturity. Now he completes the triumph over it by pointing on to the Christian hope of immortality." For God there is no time. "Thy yeeres neyther goe nor come; whereas these yeeres of ours, doe both goe and come, that (in their order) they may all come. Thy yeeres are in a standing all at once, because they are still at a stay: nor are those that goe, thrust out by those that *come,* for that they passe not away at all; but these of ours shall all bee, even when they shall not all be. Thy yeeres are one day; and thy day, is not *everyday,* but *today:* seeing thy *To day* gives not place unto *To morrowe,* nor comes in place of *yesterday*. Thy *To day* is Eternity."[208] These characteristic paradoxes are St. Augustine's. Here is Richard Baxter on *The Saints' Everlasting Rest:*[209] "Here shall I be encircled with eternity, and come forth no more: here shall I live, and ever live, and praise my Lord, and ever, ever praise him. My face will not wrinkle, nor my hair be grey. . . . The date of my lease will no more expire, nor shall I lose my joys through fear of losing them. When millions of ages are past, my glory is but beginning; and when millions more are past, it is no nearer ending. Every day is all noontide, and every month is May or harvest, and every year is there a jubilee, and every age is full manhood: and all this but one eternity."

The Book of Revelation promised this end of time, "that there should be time no longer" (10:6). Adam-Milton, gloomily looking at history, "the race of time," can hardly wait "till Time stand fixed" (12:555). "Ad Patrem" 31 had said it in Latin: "Aeternaeque morae stabunt immobilis aevi." Amaranthus was an ordinary flower in "Lycidas" 149. "Amarant" is removed to Heaven in *Paradise Lost* 3:352 and lives up to its Greek meaning of "immortal." George Herbert wished in "The Flower," "O that I once past changing were, / Fast in thy Paradise, where no flower can wither!" The Attendant Spirit in *Comus* came from the place where, according to a deleted line,[210] "eternal roses grow."

Meanwhile there is art, poetry, "making," as substitute gratification, as sublimation as well as sublimity, a mode of instinctual liberation, as bulwark against time, One cannot do better than quote Norman O. Brown[211] on—and quoting—Horace: " 'I have wrought a monument more enduring than bronze, and loftier than the royal accumulation of the pyramids. Neither corrosive rain nor raging wind can destroy it, nor the innumerable sequence of years nor the flight of time. I shall not altogether die.' I shall not altogether die—the hope of the man who has not lived, whose life has been spent conquering death, whose life has passed into those immortal pages."

In Joseph Fletcher's "discursive epic"[212] *The Historie of the Perfect-Cursed-Blessed Man* (1629)[213] are two engravings of peculiar interest. The first shows Adam strolling in Eden with his arm about his naked spouse, surrounded by sundry friendly animals, including a lion with humanoid features. Adam, it goes without saying, is in the comely prime of youth. The second engraving shows recognizably the same man, but without a spouse and afflicted by age and all the natural calamities that followed the Fall. Earthquake and fire have struck his dwelling, storm rages upon him, and the lion gnaws at his left knee, as the man, robed, sits praying. The once luxuriant hair has withered away from his brow, and his face is as lined and suffering as the familiar Faithorne engraving of Milton at sixty-two.

The last poetry Milton wrote was verses inserted in the second edition of *Paradise Lost,* 1674. In what is now Book 11 he made two additions. He added three lines to the grim list of diseases that rack men (485-87). In 551-52 he added the words, "and patiently attend my dissolution." It is like a last message, in the year of the poet's death. Milton, his work at last done, patiently awaited the end of all of him that was mortal.

Notes

References for the facts and the probabilities of Milton's life are not necessary since the publication of William Riley Parker, *Milton: A Biography,* 2 vols. (Oxford, 1968), which is up-to-date and systematic and well indexed and has 538 pages of notes and is backed by J. Milton French's *The Life Records of John Milton,* 5 vols. (New Brunswick, N.J., 1949-58). Parker also has all the relevant citations from the early biographers, of which the standard edition is edited by Helen Darbishire, *The Early Lives of Milton* (London, 1932).

Milton's text is here given the same modernization ordinarily accorded Shakespeare and the King James Bible. Reference is made to the prose and the translations of the Latin prose in the Columbia University Press edition of the *Works,* ed. Frank A. Patterson and others, 18 vols. (New York, 1931-38). For the English verse I usually follow Douglas

Bush's edition, *Complete Poetical Works* (Boston, 1965), but I have such deviations as inserting *e* rather than an apostrophe or printing *forever* instead of *for ever.* Rarely I have had my own preference in punctuation or capitalization.

1 A remark made by David Masson in his lectures. Quoted by Marjorie H. Nicolson, "Milton and the Telescope," a 1935 *ELH* article reprinted in *Science and Imagination* (Ithaca, 1956), p. 96. The quotation is repeated without attribution in Nicolson's *The Breaking of the Circle* (Evanston, 1950), p. 146. E. E. Stoll disagrees: "Time and Space in Milton," *From Shakespeare to Joyce* (New York, 1944), pp. 413-21. On the aesthetics of space-time see Jackson I. Cope, *The Metaphoric Structure of "Paradise Lost"* (Baltimore, 1962), pp. 7ff. Laurie B. Zwicky's doctoral dissertation "Milton's Use of Time" is principally concerned with *Paradise Lost* (*DA,* 20 [1959], 1030).

2 *Paradise Lost* 6:8. For a brilliant article (*pace* John R. Knott, Jr., *Milton's Pastoral Vision,* Chicago, 1971, pp. 97-98) on the recurring significance of noon and midnight, see Albert R. Cirollo, "Noon-Midnight and the Temporal Structure of *Paradise Lost,*" *ELH,* 29 (1962), 372-95; reprinted in *Critical Essays on Milton from "ELH"* (Baltimore, 1969), pp. 210-33, and in condensed form in C. A. Patrides, ed., *Milton's Epic Poetry* (Harmondsworth, 1967), pp. 215-32.

3 Strenuously denied in recent years: see the bibliography of twenty-one items in n. 3, pp. 168-69 of Balachandra Rajan, *The Lofty Rhyme* (London, 1970), to which must be added Jason R. Rosenblatt, "Adam's Pisgah Vision: *Paradise Lost,* Books XI and XII," *ELH,* 39 (1972), 66-86; Raymond B. Waddington, "The Death of Adam: Vision and Voice in Books XI and XII of *Paradise Lost,*" *MP,* 70 (1972), 9-21.

4 Georges Poulet, *Studies in Human Time,* tr. Elliott Coleman (Baltimore, 1956), pp. 13-18; Douglas Bush, *Prefaces to Renaissance Literature* (New York, 1965), pp. 65ff; Stanley Stewart, *The Enclosed Garden* (Madison, 1966), pp. 97-149. For iconography see Samuel C. Chew, *The Pilgrimage of Life* (New Haven, 1962), pp. 9-34; for philosophical or theological background, C. A. Patrides, "The Renaissance View of Time: A Bibliographical Note," *NQ,* 10 (1963), 408-10. My essay was drafted before I could see the historically very interesting book by Richard J. Quinones, *The*

Renaissance Discovery of Time (Cambridge, Mass., 1972). It turns out that there is little overlapping between my analysis (of age and youth and precocity references) and Professor Quinones's pages on Milton, 444-93. I was most fascinated by the chapter on time-conscious Petrarch (who, in contrast to Milton, "maintained throughout his life, not only in his letters and prose works, but also in his poetry an attention nothing less than astounding to exactitude in date"—p. 110) and the evidence of the popularity of the parable of the talents ("In the Renaissance, the notion of being called to account is a blend of Christian, mercantile, and classical thought"—p. 138). There are also splendid generalizations, e.g., p. 3:

> For the men of the Renaissance . . . victory over time is the measure of their heroism; a need for special distinction, one which rises above the anonymity of the everyday, compels them to seek the arduous, the unusual. Their energy and their desire for learning they contrast with the sloth and the acquiescence in ignorance which they consider to characterize their predecessors and contemporaries. It is important to observe that for most of the writers discussed in this study, for Petrarch, for Rabelais, for Shakespeare, and for Milton, it is precisely this new sense of time, calling forth energetic, even heroic response, that they use to distinguish themselves and the leaders of their new age from the preceding age.

5 *Paradise Lost* 9:26.

6 *John Milton, Englishman* (New York, 1949), p. 12. Cf. Harris F. Fletcher, *The Intellectual Development of John Milton*, (Urbana, 1956), I, 74, 90, 427-28; Donald L. Clark, *John Milton at St. Paul's School* (New York, 1948), pp. 29-30.

7 Columbia *Works,* XII, 325.

8 "At a Vacation Exercise" 1-6. Coleridge's comment: "Well might He speak late who spoke to such purpose!" (Ed. J. A. Wittreich, Jr., *The Romantics on Milton* [Cleveland, 1970], p. 265.)

9 *Paradise Regained* 4:220.

10 Reproduced in color as the frontispiece of the Columbia *Works.*

11 *Works,* VIII, 119.

12 Hanford, p. 14.

13 *P.R.* 1:201ff.

14 Ibid., 3:31.

15 There is always the possibility of a misprinted numeral. I instance only the two proven cases, but others are suspect. See the pioneering article by Parker, "Some Problems in the Chronology of Milton's Early Poems," *RES,* 11 (1935), 276-83.

16 See the notes to letters numbered 1, 4, 7, 8, 9 (discussed II, 760), and 11 in the Yale *Complete Prose Works,* general editor Don M. Wolfe (New Haven), I (1953), II (1959).

17 See Parker, *Milton,* p. 827, n. 39.

18 *Works,* VIII, 126. S. B. Liljegren (*Studies in Milton,* originally Lund, 1918; reprinted New York, 1967, p. 16, n. 2) noted the discrepancy, which Masson had overlooked. Liljegren inferred that Milton was a liar. I infer that Milton did not have a good memory for personal dates, for a reason that I conjecture. See further B. A. Wright, "The Alleged Falsehoods in Milton's Account of His Continental Tour," *MLR,* 28 (1933), 308-14, whose apologetic interpretation of Milton's Latin seems strained. He takes the ablative absolute "rupta pace" as "the key phrase" and "redintegrebat" as meaning, "the King, having broken the Peace, was preparing to renew the war" (313-14).

19 John Toland, in Darbishire, p. 179. Repeated by Richardson, ibid., p. 211.

20 "Milton has carefully stressed the youthfulness of the four opening poems," says Louis L. Martz, "The Rising Poet," in *The Lyric and Dramatic Milton,* ed. J. H. Summers (New York, 1965), p. 21, but the reader, not knowing when the poet was born, knew only that the Nativity Ode was written a certain number of years ago. Since, in Martz's own words, the frontispiece "presents the harsh and crabbed image of a man who might be forty or fifty" (p. 6), although the legend in the oval said at some unknown time he was twenty-one, there was little to discourage the conjecture that Milton might have been middle-aged in 1629.

21 *The Reason of Church Government, Works,* III, 235.

22 Parker, *Milton,* p. 289.

23 See the table in Fletcher, II (Urbana, 1961), 43.

24 *Considerations, Works,* VI, 92.

25 Elegia I, 11, 14. "Phoebicolis" being a most unusual formation, of which Walter MacKellar knows no example and

Douglas Bush (see his annotation for *A Variorum Commentary* on *The Latin and Greek Poems,* I, 49, New York, 1970) only one, in Joseph Scaliger, it is worth noting that the word turns up on p. 1 of the Latin section of *Justa Edouardo King,* 1638 (New York, Facsimile Text Society, 1939), in the poem by Nicholas Felton.

26 *Works,* III, 304.

27 *Works,* XII, 121.

28 *An Apology for Smectymnuus, Works,* III, 300.

29 *Works,* XII, 241.

30 *Works,* XII, 213.

31 Donald C. Dorian, *The English Diodatis* (New Brunswick, 1950), pp. 108-9.

32 Prolusio III, *Works,* XII, 160.

33 *Church Government, Works,* III, 236.

34 "The Passion" 5.

35 *Works,* XII, 291.

36 Bush, *Variorum,* pp. 11-13, 333ff. Sir Toby Belch remembered "diluculo surgere" from his Latin grammar (*Twelfth Night* II.iii.2). In Petrarch's *De Remediis* (I.i, cited by Quinones, p. 147) Ratio cries out, "Expergiscimini, consopiti: tempus est, caligantesque oculos aperite!"

37 Prolusio I, *Works,* XII, 141.

38 J. Dover Wilson, *Life in Shakespeare's England* (Harmondsworth, 1944), pp. 347, 349.

39 Darbishire, ed., Milton's *Poetical Works,* II (Oxford, 1966), p. 308.

40 *Works,* XII, 145-47.

41 *Church Government, Works,* III, 224.

42 "Epitaphium Damonis" 54.

43 Prolusio VI, *Works,* XII, 241.

44 *P.L.* 9:1049.

45 *Works,* XII, 65.

46 *Observations on the Articles of Peace, Works,* VI, 264.

47 *Tenure of Kings, Works,* V, 44.

48 *Observations, Works,* VI, 267.

49 2:227.

50 10:1055.

51 5:673; cf. 38.

52 1:331.

53 Kingsley Widmer, "The Iconography of Renunciation: The Miltonic Simile," in Patrides, *Milton's Epic Poetry,* p. 128.

54 Letter to Gill dated 4 December 1634 as translated by John Carey in Carey and Alastair Fowler, ed., *Poems* (London, 1968), p. 229.

55 *Apology for Smectymnuus, Works,* III, 298-99.

56 *Works,* VI, 330.

57 5:20.

58 Henry John Todd, ed., Milton's *Poetical Works,* 5th edition (London, 1852), IV, 269.

59 *Musophilus,* 27ff. (in *Poetry of the English Renaissance,* ed. J. W. Hebel and H. H. Hudson [New York, 1929], p. 267). Two useful and independent essays on Milton and fame are M. Y. Hughes, "Milton and the Sense of Glory," *PQ,* 28 (1949), 107-24; M. M. Mahood, *Poetry and Humanism* (London, 1950), pp. 225ff.

60 See ch. 3, "The Translation of the Myth: The Epicedia and 'Lycidas'," of Don Cameron Allen's *The Harmonious Vision* (Baltimore, 1954); Michael West, "The *Consolatio* in Milton's Funeral Elegies," *HLQ,* 34 (1971), 233-49.

61 30ff.; "At a Solemn Music" 25ff.

62 "The attitude is oddly but appropriately expressive of the sentiments of young academic gentlemen toward those minor functionaries who are ridiculed during their lives and offices only to have it faintly remembered at their passing that they were human." Hanford, "The Youth of Milton," in University of Michigan *Studies in Shakespeare, Milton and Donne* (New York, 1925), p. 100.

63 See his recapitulation in refutation of Sirluck in *Milton,* pp. 784-87. Parker's date is accepted in the Columbia *Variorum,* II, ed. Woodhouse and Bush (New York, 1972), pp. 354ff. The Marchioness of Winchester and Turgarus (*Works,* X, 243) references are Parker's.

64 *Works,* XV, 34.

65 20-22. Cf. *Romaunt of the Rose,* 369, 371 (pp. 62 and 569 of Chaucer's *Works,* ed. F. N. Robinson, 2nd edition [Boston, 1957]; cf. the note to line 20, p. 690).

66 Robert Baron, *Pocula Castalia,* 1650, p. 27, quoted

by Todd ad loc. (e.g., in his first edition of the *Poetical Works,* London, 1801, V, 460).

67 Sonnet 70. I do not very well see the connection with Spenser's Latin verse letter to Gabriel Harvey (1580) suggested by Roland M. Smith, "Spenser and Milton: An Early Analogue," *MLN,* 60 (1945), 394-98.

68 Cited by Hughes, ed., Milton's *Complete Poems and Major Prose* (New York, 1957), p. 76. The citations from Seneca, Chaucer, Shakespeare, Randolph's and Herrick's "envious time," and, in detail, Cowley (a name first connected with the sonnet by Gosse and Grosart and revived in my *Milton Dictionary,* New York, 1961, p. 301) are mine.

69 "L'Allegro" 133; "On Shakespeare" 9.

70 *John Milton, Englishman,* p. 67.

71 G. Thorn-Drury, ed., *The Poems of Thomas Randolph* (London, 1929), p. vii.

72 "To Time," attributed to Randolph, p. 163.

73 Hanford, *John Milton, Englishman,* p. 63. Todd's 1798 edition of *Comus* (Canterbury) cited Randolph at 1. 710. See, further, the Columbia *Variorum,* II, 773-75.

74 "An Elegie on the death of my loving Friend and Cousen, Master Richard Clerke" 24, p. 41 of Abraham Cowley, *Essays, Plays and Sundry Verses,* ed. A. R. Waller (Cambridge, 1906). Same phrase in Robert Herrick, "His Poetry His Pillar" 20.

75 "A popular work issued in December would very likely bear the date of the following year." W. W. Greg, *Collected Papers,* ed. J. C. Maxwell (Oxford, 1966), p. 372. The conjectures of A. H. Nethercot were based on two questionable assumptions: 1. that Milton's sonnet belongs to 1631; 2. that Cowley's book did not come out until 1633 (*Abraham Cowley, The Muse's Hannibal* [London, 1931], pp. 22-23; "Milton, Jonson, and Young Cowley," *MLN,* 49 [1934], 158-62).

76 Ed. cit., p. 30.

77 His widow declared his favorite poets were Cowley, Shakespeare, Spenser. A. B. Grosart in his edition of Cowley's *Complete Works* (Edinburgh, 1881), I, xliii, saw "Even so I sported with her Beauties light /Till I at last grew blind with too much sight" ("Constantia and Philetus," stanza 50) as the possible source of "Dark with excessive bright thy

skirts appear," *P.L.* 3:380. There is a monograph by Rudolph Kirsten, *Studie über das Verhältnis von Cowley and Milton* (Meiningen, 1889), which mainly deals with the relation between the *Davideis* and *P.L.*, but which, p. 15, connects the sonnet with stanza 11 of "A Vote" and, p. 18, "At a Vacation Exercise" 19-20 with stanza 7.

78 As Douglas Bush's headnote (ed., *Complete Poetical Works,* pp. 104-5) summarizes, "He had become a literary and intellectual figure in the Cambridge world, but now he has been for six months an obscure student under his father's roof, beginning the years of hard reading by which he hoped to prepare himself for the unknown future; meanwhile his contemporaries are forging ahead."

79 Included in the Carey and Fowler edition of Milton's *Poems,* p. 254, with a correction of the surely wrong reading "overdaled."

80 *Works,* III, 1, 469; V, 185.

81 12:553ff, quoted by E. A. J. Honigmann, ed., *Milton's Sonnets* (London, 1966), pp. 97-98.

82 *Works,* VIII, 61.

83 John S. Smart, ed., *The Sonnets of Milton* (Glasgow, 1921), p. 54.

84 "The Youth of Milton," p. 128.

85 Ibid., pp. 112-13.

86 D. C. Dorian, *Explicator,* 8 (1949), item 10.

87 Above "seated." See *Facsimile of the Manuscript of Milton's Minor Poems,* ed. W. A. Wright (Cambridge, 1899), p. 7.

88 37-43, tr. Sir J. E. Sandys in the Loeb Library, 1915. The comparison was made by L. Campbell in the *Classical Review,* 8 (1894), 349.

89 Prolusio VII, *Works,* XII 249.

90 *A Midsummer Night's Dream* V.i.13.

91 *Works,* XII, 255.

92 A range of attitudes is found by looking up "aetas" in such standard reference works as *Thesaurus Linguae Latinae,* Harper's *Latin Dictionary,* and *Paulys Real-Encyclopädie der Classischen Altertumswissenschaft.* P. 1129 of the *Thesaurus* gloomily quotes Irenaeus (2:22:5): "a quadrigesimo et quinquagesimo anno declinat iam in aetatem

seniorem." On the Ages of Man (figures sometimes given) see Chew, pp. 144-73.

93 *Works,* XII, 11.

94 *Life of William Shakespeare* (London, 1915), p. 155.

95 *The Affectionate Shepherd* in A. H. Bullen, *Some Longer Elizabethan Poems* (Westminster, 1903), p. 169. It is only fair to say that Barnfield is speaking in the persona of Daphnis.

96 *Idea,* 43 (1599). (44 in *Works,* ed. J. W. Hebel [Oxford, 1932], II, 332).

97 *Idea,* 14 (1594). *Works,* ed. Hebel, I, 104.

98 "To the truly Noble Sir Robert Ker, afterwards Earl of Ancrum" (Drummond's *Works,* Edinburgh, 1711, p. 143).

99 *Works,* XII, 249.

100 On this subject see Frederick C. Prescott, *The Poetic Mind* (New York, 1922), ch. 2, "Examples of Vision." Incidentally, in this section I am pilfering some words and references from my *Endymion in England: The Literary History of a Greek Myth* (New York, 1944), pp. 126–27. On the psychoanalytic meaning of caves, see Norman O. Brown, *Love's Body* (New York, 1966), ch. 2, with references, especially G. Roheim.

101 Drayton, "Fourth Eglogue," *Works,* ed. Hebel, II, 533.

102 See, further, Bush's *Variorum* note (p. 99) on Elegia V, 17.

103 *De Augmentis Scientiarum,* II, ch. 13, in *Works,* ed. Spedding, Ellis, Heath (Boston, 1863), VIII, 456-57.

104 Rose Macaulay, *Milton* (London, 1957), p. 46.

105 "Matthew Arnold's New Poems" in *Essays and Studies* (London, 1875), p. 155.

106 *Justa Edouardo King,* pp. 33-34. It is true that the prefatory prose panegyric headed "P.M.S." (Poeta Miltonius Scripsit?) says of King, "IN QUO NIHIL IMMATURUM PRAETER AETATEM."

107 *Works,* IV, 279.

108 *Works,* X, 203.

109 E. M. W. Tillyard, *Milton* (New York, 1967), pp. 71-72.

110 "But if they desire to see other countries at three or

four and twenty years of age . . ." *Works,* IV, 290.

111 Ecloga VII, 27-28. To get away from the misleading translation of "futuro" as "destined" or "predestined" favored by Miltonists, I quote the translation by the eminent Virgilian (who also wrote about Milton) J. W. Mackail, *Virgil's Works* (New York, 1934, Modern Library), p. 282. Thyrsis and Corydon are both young ("ambo florentes aetatibus," 4) and developing ("crescentem . . . poetam," 25).

112 *De Officiis* II 13 (the section on attaining glory). "Those who pass their early years unknown to man in humbleness and obscurity should, as soon as they approach manhood, have their eye on greatness and strive towards it with steady zeal, which they will do with a firmer mind because that time of life is not only not subject to envy but even favored" ("quia non modo non invidetur illi aetati, verum etiam favetur"). Even the *Areopagitica* contains an *absit invidia* formula (*Works,* IV, 330): "I might say, if without envy . . . "

113 Note appended to "The Passion."

114 "Milton in Rustication," *SP,* 19 (1922), 121-22.

115 Tr. Nelson G. McCrea in *The Student's Milton,* ed. Frank A. Patterson (New York, 1933), p. 109.

116 "Ad Patrem" 115; *Works,* III, 235.

117 *Works,* III, 241.

118 *Works,* IV, 12.

119 86. "Annorumque satur cineri sua jura relinquam."

120 *Works,* III, 183.

121 See Parker, *Milton's Contemporary Reputation* (Columbus, 1940), p. 73, for the quotation from Bishop John Bramhall, 1643.

122 *Works,* III, 232.

123 Ibid., 234.

124 Ibid., 238.

125 *Works,* III, 283.

126 *Works,* III, 282. I have concluded elsewhere from the poignant first words quoted that "Milton is feeling doubts and strains that will shortly—in a matter of weeks—impel him to marriage." "Milton Remembers *The Praise of Folly,*" *PMLA,* 71 (1956), 840.

127 *The Eloquent "I": Style and Self in Seventeenth-*

Century Prose (Madison, 1968), p. 214. The other commentator I alluded to is Ralph A. Haug, who has a summarizing note to *Reason of Church Government* in the Yale *Complete Prose,* I, 806, n. 37. (Milton was not, however, "twenty" when the "Fair Infant" died.) Incidentally, Carey's objection in Carey and Fowler (eds.), p. 14, that "two-year-old Anne cannot have been the poem's subject, since the 'infant' of whom M. writes did not outlast even a single winter (3-4)" is fallacious. The infant did not outlast *that* winter, its second.

128 *Works,* III, 343.

129 *Works,* IV, 301.

130 *The Judgment of Martin Bucer Touching Divorce, Works,* IV, 17.

131 The first chapter of Hanford's biography is entitled "Christ among the Doctors."

132 Edward Phillips, in Darbishire, *Early Lives,* p. 70.

133 *Works,* VIII, 101.

134 See Fletcher, I, 74.

135 Yale *Complete Prose,* IV (1966), 963.

136 Ibid., 315.

137 *Works,* VII, 66. Cf. "veterator," 240; "veteratorie," 130.

138 *Works,* VIII, 31.

139 *Works,* IX, 281. The same words were used in Prolusio VII: "velut occulto aevo crescere" (*Works,* XII, 248-50).

140 The sonnets and the letter were connected in an interesting essay by Macon Cheek, "Of Two Sonnets of Milton," reprinted in Arthur E. Barker, ed., *Milton: Modern Essays in Criticism* (New York, 1965), pp. 125-35.

141 *Works,* IV, 278.

142 *Works,* X, 248.

143 *Works,* X, 236.

144 *The Ready and Easy Way to Establish a Free Commonwealth, Works,* VI, 136.

145 *Works,* III, 241; X, 79.

146 "It appears incredible that Milton's great plea for freedom of the press should have failed of any mention whatever in the thousands of pages printed at the time and abounding in specific references to hundreds of other publications,

but the present writer is constrained to report that after a protracted search he has failed to find a single one." William Haller, ed., *Tracts on Liberty in the Puritan Revolution* (New York, 1934), I, 134. But see Yale *Complete Prose*, II, 87.

147 *Works,* IV, 272. "Disappointment at the reception of the *Doctrine and Discipline of Divorce* may have influenced Milton to collect his poems together for the volume he published in 1645." Alan Rudrum, ed., *Milton: Modern Judgements* (London, 1968), p. 11. Cf. Parker, *Milton,* p. 288.

148 The fullest account is in David Masson, *The Life of John Milton* (reprinted New York, 1946), III, 189-92.

149 *Works,* VIII, 114; letter to Leo van Aitzema of 5 February 1655, *Works,* XII, 72.

150 *Works,* XII, 47.

151 Ibid., 51.

152 *Milton,* p. 353.

153 *Works,* VI, 267.

154 *Works,* IV, 281; compare "led to the praxis thereof in some chosen short book lessoned thoroughly to them." 278.

155 *Works,* VI, 78.

156 Compare John Donne's Sonnet (17) on his deceased wife, "Since she whom I lov'd hath payd her last debt / To Nature, and to hers, and my good is dead."

157 *Works,* V, 63.

158 Ibid., 219.

159 Ibid., 309.

160 Ibid., 67.

161 Ibid., 64.

162 Ibid., 65.

163 Ibid., 83.

164 Ibid., 308.

165 "To Mr. Cyriack Skinner Upon his Blindness." "Rings" is one of the 1694 variants.

166 *Works,* XII, 65.

167 With reference to the first, Hanford, *John Milton, Englishman,* wrote p. 11: "His later insistence on the idea that thoroughness of preparation is more important than speed of progress sounds to me like a rationalization of events injurious to his self-confidence in early life, though success-

fully compensated by intellectual achievement."

168 *Milton,* p. 307.

169 Ibid., p. 314.

170 In *An Entertainment of King and Queen at Theobalds, Works,* ed. C. H. Herford and P. Simpson (Oxford, 1925-52), VII, 154.

171 The best alternative explanation is D. C. Dorian's, interpreting "days" as "working days," *Explicator,* 10 (1951), item 16.

172 "To the Lady Margaret Ley" 8; also referred to in *Of Education, Works,* IV, 287 and of course *Areopagitica.*

173 John T. Shawcross, "Milton's Sonnet 19," *NQ,* n.s. 4 (1957), 442-46, and in his editions, *The Complete English Poetry* (New York, 1963), p. 215, and *The Complete Poetry* (New York, 1971), p. 242. See further, Columbia *Variorum Commentary,* II, 464.

174 I, ch. 8 (*Works,* XV, 91).

175 Ibid., 93.

176 John Carey, *Milton* (London, 1969), p. 74.

177 *Works,* VIII, 60.

178 Ibid., 21.

179 Ibid., 19.

180 Ibid.

181 *Works,* VIII, 113.

182 *Works,* VII, 555.

183 *The Ready and Easy Way, Works,* VI, 116.

184 *Works,* VII, 559.

185 *Milton,* p. 473.

186 *Works,* XII, 333.

187 *Works,* VI, 44.

188 Parker italicizes *"the marvel is that the drama was ever printed,"* "The Date of *Samson Agonistes,*" *PQ,* 28 (1949), 150-51.

189 *Apology, Works,* III, 342. Sir John Suckling's letter to Thomas Carew, advising, "Well, if thou must needs marry, . . . let it be a maid and no widow," had not yet been printed. The letter, with Carew's dissenting answer, is in A. M. Witherspoon and F. J. Warnke, ed., *Seventeenth-Century Prose and Poetry* (New York, 1963), pp. 435-36.

190 See "Uric Acid and the Psyche," *Journal of the American Medical Association,* 208 (19 May 1969), 1180. This recent conclusion, too new to be in Edward A. Block's article "Milton's Gout," *Bulletin of the History of Medicine,* 28 (1954), 201-11, naturally invites reflection on other gout sufferers, such as Edmund Wilson.

191 By Alan H. Gilbert, *PQ,* 28 (1949), 98-106.

192 Shawcross, a former student of Parker's, supports these heresies with a statistical analysis of prosody in "The Chronology of Milton's Major Poems," *PMLA,* 76 (1961), 345-58. One ready objection must be that Milton is given nothing to do between 1663, or 1665, and 1671 (and too much to do at an earlier period).

193 "Milton's Crises," a review of Parker's *Milton, Listener,* 19 December 1968, p. 829.

194 When "we have submitted to the conditions of the conqueror, we must lay down our pens as well as arms." Quoted in Nethercot, *Abraham Cowley,* pp. 158-59.

195 "Life of Cowley," in *Works* (Oxford, 1825), VII, 44.

196 "First Epistle of the Second Book of Horace" 75.

197 In Darbishire, *Early Lives,* p. 276.

198 Northrop Frye, *The Return of Eden* (Toronto, 1965), p. 5. Coleridge was to say, "I should not think of devoting less than 20 years to an Epic Poem. Ten to collect materials and warm my mind with universal science. I would be a tolerable Mathematician, I would thoroughly know Mechanics, Hydrostatics, Optics, and Astronomy, Botany, Metallurgy, Fossilism, Chemistry, Geology, Anatomy, Medicine—then the *mind of man*—then the *minds of men*—in all Travels, Voyages and Histories. So I would spend ten years—the next five to the composition of the poem—and the five last to the correction of it." Wittreich, p. 159. Edward Wagenknecht suggests as "the basic reason for [Milton's] late development as a poet—that he had to reconcile his Hellenism with his Hebraism" (*The Personality of Milton* [Norman, 1970], p. 57). Cf. Wordsworth's conclusion, "However imbued the surface might be with classical literature, he was a Hebrew in soul." When Milton wrote *Samson Agonistes,* "his mind was Hebraized. Indeed, his genius fed on the writings of the Hebrew prophets. This arose, in some degree, from the

temper of the times; the Puritan lived in the Old Testament, almost to the exclusion of the New" (Wittreich, pp. 130, 136).

199 Holbrook Jackson, ed. (London, 1932, Everyman's Library), I, 26.

200 New York, Heritage Press, 1948, p. xl.

201 Rajan, p. 128.

202 12:611. *Iliad* 1:63.

203 As an undergraduate summarized, Milton is "whistling in the dark." John Dorling, University of East Anglia, Norwich, in John Broadbent, *"Paradise Lost": Introduction* (Cambridge, 1972), p. 84.

204 *Works,* V, 65. Six parallel quotations are given in my *Yet Once More: Verbal and Psychological Pattern in Milton* (New York, 1953; reprinted, 1969), pp. 121-22.

205 *Milton* (London, 1957), p. 84.

206 *Works,* VIII, 399; Commentary, XI, 150.

207 "Notes on Milton's Early Development," *UTQ,* 13 (1943), 97-98 (same statement in *The Heavenly Muse: A Preface to Milton,* Toronto, 1972, p. 53).

208 Augustine's *Confessions* 11:13, tr. William Watts, 1651, pp. 753-54, as quoted by Rosalie L. Colie, "Time and Eternity: Paradox and Structure in *Paradise Lost,*" JWCI, 23 (1960), 129. As Patrides and others have pointed out, however, Milton does not consciously subscribe to this "eternal present" view. Cf. pp. 49-53 of Barbara Lewalski's "Time and History in *Paradise Regained*" in Rajan, ed., *The Prison and the Pinnacle* (Toronto, 1973).

209 Ed. John Wesley (New York, 1843), p. 316.

210 W. A. Wright, ed., *Facsimile,* p. 10.

211 *Life against Death* (Middletown, 1959), p. 287 (*Odes* 3:30). Milton's earliest echo of the Horatian tag is "On Shakespeare" 8.

212 Following the classification of Burton O. Kurth, *Milton and Christian Heroism: Biblical Epic Themes and Forms in Seventeenth-Century England* (Berkeley, 1959), p. 137. PL-213 in Watson Kirkconnell, *The Celestial Cycle: The Theme of Paradise Lost in World Literature* (Toronto, 1952).

213 Figures 23 and 24 in Stewart, *The Enclosed Garden.*

AREOPAGITICA AS A SCENARIO FOR *PARADISE LOST*

II

Modern commentators have done much to bring Milton's prose closer to his verse. Tillyard and Grierson and Hutchinson, taking a hint from Milton himself, declared that the *Defensio Secunda* has some qualities of an epic.[1] Haller saw *Comus* as the Puritan sermon that its author never mounted a pulpit to deliver.[2] Lines 108-31 of "Lycidas" must be counted, obviously, as the first antiprelatical tract. Barker makes a literally picturesque connection: "Episcopacy assumed in his eyes the lineaments of Comus; it was the public manifestation of the perversions of carnal sensuality against which he had striven in favor of high seriousness. The reformed discipline of the Puritan church similarly assumed the aspect of the virgin Lady, possessed of transcendent spiritual powers."[3] Backing this observation lies G. Wilson Knight's,[4] published the same year: "A great poet rarely modifies his primary impressionisms, but, using them as constants, gears them to the ever-changing world of his experience." The Yale editors of *Of Reformation*[5] point out in their first footnote that that prose debut is one extended metaphor. As part of his argument that *Samson Agonistes* was a composition of Milton's second period, Parker gave seven pages of exact verbal parallels with the 1640s prose.[6]

Areopagitica is not part of a pamphlet war, like the 1641-42 episcopal assaults. It is not a tractate. As oratory it is one of the "organic arts" that Milton had linked with poetry a few months before.[7] "According to the theory of poetry that Milton accepted, the poet and the orator share the desire to move men to virtuous action. Persuasion, the chief end of oratory, is also part of the function of poetry."[8] The outstanding authorities have, of course, noticed the change from the preceding tracts. Haller[9] thinks "Milton wrote not a pamphlet but a poem." Wolfe sees "a broad humanism fresh as the spirit of Plato's praise of music or Sidney's paeans for poetry."[10] Barker[11] is reminded of the Nativity Ode.

It seems, then, a question of just what poetry Milton had in mind. The present essay aims to provide detail to Tillyard's[12] statement: "*Areopagitica* looked back to the once planned Arthuriad; it also contained hints of *Paradise Lost.*" Tillyard is very brief in his discussion of *Areopagitica,* perhaps feeling that it had been gone over too much already. In fact the remark just quoted occurs in his chapter on *Defensio Secunda.* Also it is still possible to contribute some fresh annotations to the relevant passages.

Of course both *Areopagitica* and *Paradise Lost* deal with the limits of freedom, which was always Milton's subject. Both works portray temptation.

Areopagitica is not lacking in the personages of *Paradise Lost.* It has, more than once, Adam (Columbia *Works,* IV, 311, 319) (and by implication, or association, Eve). It has "an angel" (307) or two. It has Lucifer (353). There is even a snake (344). And there is the snake's favorite vegetable, fennel (*Paradise Lost* 9:581), in the form of "the ferular" (324), which is the giant fennel. There are "limbos,"[13] "hells," and "damned" (305).

Knowing that Milton had behind him four outlines for a tragedy on the *Paradise Lost* theme, knowing that he had already written ten lines of what became Book 4 of the epic,[14] we have some licence to make the experiment of describing the future poem in phrases taken entirely from *Areopagitica*. There is, first, the poet who, though "stark blind" (339) and facing up to the possibility of being "the worst for two-and-fifty degrees of northern latitude" (296; compare the "cold climate" of 9:44-45), but "with hope," "with confidence" "at the beginning of no mean endeavor" (293), and not unmindful of the prospect of "lasting fame" (323; same phrase as at 3:449), receives "the dictate of a divine Spirit" (326). He "justifies the high Providence of God" (320) "to that hapless race of men" (327). Lucifer, "fallen from the stars" (353), is still the "subtlest enemy of our faith" (307). "He of the bottomless pit . . . broke prison" (304); it is not given even to the angels to "bar him down" (304); he has passed "doors which cannot be shut" (328; cf. 2:883-84), "custody" of "all the locks and keys" (334; "the fatal key," 2:725,871) not having been faithfully kept. Gabriel, rather futilely, is assigned to guard Paradise, "to walk the round and counter-round with his fellow inspectors, fearing lest any of his flock be seduced" (336).

As "the trial of virtue" (320; "matter of glorious trial," 9:1177), "a dangerous and suspicious fruit" (306), indeed "the rind of one apple tasted" (310), proves too much for the first couple, largely on account of Eve's insistence that she "may walk abroad without a keeper" (328). Unwarily they underrated the difficulty of obeying God, "whose command perhaps made all things seem easy and unlaborious to them" (322; compare Adam's first speech to Eve: "This easy charge . . . let us not think hard/ One easy prohibition" [4:421,432-33]). " 'Tis . . . alleged we must not expose ourselves to temptations without necessity" (315). Raphael teaches that we "not employ our time in vain things" (315). But the Fall has taken place, the way is open from Hell "to scout into the regions of sin" (311), and nothing is left now but to await and prophesy "the end of mortal things" (349; "mortal things," 1:693), while noting that there are times when "God . . . raises to his own work men of rare abilities" (350).

"Lasting fame" and "mortal things" are but two of the phrases in *Areopagitica* to be found in *Paradise Lost*. "The bottomless pit" is Revelation (9:1,2,11; 11:7; 17:8; 20:1,3); it is also *Paradise Lost* 6:866. "Beatific vision" (336) becomes "vision beatific" (1:684). T. Holt White in 1819[15] observed that the words in the opening sentence, "not a little altered and moved inwardly in their minds" (293), with the mention of "passion" in the next sentence, come out twenty-odd years later as "works in the mind no change" and "unmoved" (8:525,532)—the effect of the regular pleasures of Paradise in contrast to Adam's "passion" (8:529) for Eve, as confessed to Raphael. From the passion of oratory to the passion of copulation, "transported touch" (8:530), it is a singular but verbally recognizable connection. Moreover, to mention what has not been noticed, Milton in the same places associates "joy and gratulation" (293): "The Earth/ Gave sign of gratulation, and each hill;/ Joyous the birds" (8:513-15). And the futility of "this cautelous enterprise of licencing" is apparently to be compared with the crafty conspiracy of Lucifer in Heaven, "vain and impossible attempts" (314), "vain attempt" (1:44).[16]

A most interesting resemblance in this class was noticed by Tillyard,[17] who saw the statement that "God . . . gives us minds that can wander beyond all limit and satiety" (320) as anticipatory of Belial's argument against annihilation, "for who would lose . . . Those thoughts that wander through eternity" . . . (2:146,148).[18] God's bounty in the prose sentence includes what the rebellious angels have just lost: "pours out before us even to a profuseness all desirable things" (the original spelling is "powrs," suggesting a pun, *powers*). Belial, the intellectual, clings to his mind as all that he has left. He fancies *it* has not been made captive. There is irony, if not poignance, here.[19] In actuality the formerly angelic mind has lost its intuitive power and can no longer be sure of the truth, "in wand'ring mazes lost" (2:561). "Wander beyond all limit"; "found no end, in wand'ring mazes": there is a parallel, too (to wander is to err), reflecting the author's impatience with scholastic abstractions. He is such a "materialist"[20] that, as we have seen, his own metaphors become literal or mythic. But his message will continue to be that truth is a hard quest.

Postponing consideration of another central message, "Reason is but choosing" (319), "Reason also is choice" (3:108), we need to give some attention to the exordium of *Areopagitica* as it compares to the proem to *Paradise Lost*. The *furor poeticus* of the exordium, with its disjointed syntax, its inserted qualifications—it begins with an anacoluthon and the reader has to keep a sharp eye out for the antecedent of a "which" or an "it," or the subject of "likely might"—is highly characteristic. The orator, as he depicts his own attitudes, is endeavoring to wind his audience into a receptive frame of mind. He does not feel unworthy, but he must not sound proud. It is necessary to compliment Parliament but not to be taken for a flatterer.[21] It is a difficult course to steer, and the ship rocks before it steadies. There is just enough uneasiness to conjure up someone else whose "appeal is a skillful union of logical machinery . . . and rhetorical insinuation." So a recent critic characterizes the speech of—Belial.[22]

But it is St. Paul whose shoes Milton, as teacher or preacher, is filling in going "unto Areopagus" (Acts 17:19), even as he associated himself with Moses at the beginning of his epic. The commentators, concentrating on Isocrates, have overlooked the certainty that the other orator on Ares' Hill would have been not only in Milton's mind[23] but the obvious first thought of his readers. All these knew the Bible better than any other book, and only some of them knew the Greek rhetorician, whom, in fact, *Areopagitica* never names, as it does name, more than once, St. Paul. (Indeed Milton was indulging his usual tendency to be "rather too academic and isolated to catch the public ear."[24]) The title page has nothing of Isocrates: rather a quotation from Euripides. There is no particular resemblance between Isocrates' oration and Milton's. The feminine form of Milton's title, whether considered as an adjective, which it properly is, or a noun, does not fit

Isocrates' *Logos Areiopagitikos*. It looks as if the English arguer is much more concerned with drawing an analogy between the "High Court of Parliament" (so his opening words designate it, 293, and his title page reads "To the Parlament of England") and the high court of Athens, a court that functioned for centuries and that Paul addressed[25] and Isocrates did not. We need only grasp the implications of the facts as stated by R. C. Jebb:[26] "The *Areopagiticus* of Isocrates (355 B.C.) is a speech, supposed to be made in the ekklesia, *about t*he Areiopagos—urging the restoration of its old powers. The *Areopagitica* of Milton is a speech *to* the English Areiopagos." The title *Areopagitica: A Speech* translates into Latin as *Areopagitica Oratio*. The author, in two Latin references, using his title as a noun, is still careful to keep the other noun nearby: "Areopagitica, sive de libertate Typographiae Oratio"; ". . . . ad justae orationis modum Areopagiticam scripsi."[27]

He "who from his private house wrote that discourse to the Parliament of Athens" (296, referring to the *ekklesia,* not the *Areopagos*) does not get alluded to until page three, and then never again—just the one sentence. Besides, he is just the first example of "a private orator" (296), Dion Prusaeus being another. But "Moses, Daniel, and Paul" are joined, six pages further on, as "skilful in . . . learning" (306), and "Paul especially" (306) singled out, not without a reference to that very chapter in Acts (17) that relates how "Paul stood in the midst of Mars' Hill, and said, Ye men of Athens, I perceive that in all things ye are too superstitious" (22). This is the accusation that Milton, with such tact as he can manage, is directing at an English Parliament that has gone papistical in its restraint of the press. The word "superstition" is significantly planted on his very first page (294). Dionysius the Areopagite was so called because he was a follower of Paul (Acts 17:34); so is Milton.

How much Milton felt like St. Paul, whom he quoted more than a dozen times in *Areopagitica,*[28] ranks among difficult questions such as to what extent he identified with Jesus in *Paradise Regained.* He had, like Dante, a habit of grouping himself with the best: when blind, with the great blind. If Isocrates was a poor orator for physical reasons, so Paul admitted it was said of himself that "his bodily presence is weak and his speech contemptible" (2 Corinthians 10:10). Milton, still obscure and having won nothing but attack lately, had the complex of imagining the breaking through from obscurity to "sudden blaze."[29] This becomes one part of his affinity with Moses as the poet mounts again, Horeb and Sinai, for as stated in the previous essay, it is to be remembered that the author of the Pentateuch was "slow of speech" (Exodus 4:10) until kindled by the Lord, even as the author of *Paradise Lost* was "long choosing, and beginning late" (9:26). Parker is the latest of Milton's biographers to comment, "It was his destiny to be slow in development."[30]

Whatever sort of speaker Milton was—about which we have no information—he does show in *Defensio Secunda*[31] some defensiveness in regard to his very middling height, which may have been one of the reasons he was called "Lady" at Christ's College. The anonymous biographer reported he "was of a moderate stature," but Aubrey indicated he was less than that.[32] *Areopagitica* thrusts forward an interesting but rather gratuitous comparison with Truth as at first "unsightly and unplausible" (Milton with his innovative doctrines?) "even as the person is of many a great man slight and contemptible to see to" (350). "Contemptible" returns us to the St. Paul quotation, but to what degree, if any, is Milton thinking of himself? There is the verbal parallel with "a certain Shepherd Lad" in *Comus* 619-20, "Of small regard to see to, yet well skilled," who Hanford argued was Milton.[33] "Person...of many a great man slight" comes back in *Defensio Secunda* when Milton is defending himself against the personal abuse of the *Regii Sanguinis Clamor:* "Sed quid si parva, qua et summi saepe tum pace tum bello viri fuere? quanquam parva dicitur, quae ad virtutem satis magna est?"[34] The author's motto, twice chosen for an autograph album, was the Pauline "My strength is made perfect in weakness."[35]

Leaving venturesome biographical conjecture, we come next to a passage that weirdly looks forward to Sin's tale to Satan of, first, Death's birth and, next, Death's incestuous rape that produced the hell-hounds that continuously ravage her:

> . . . The Council of Trent and the Spanish Inquisition, engendering together, brought forth, or perfected those Catalogues and expurging[36] Indexes that rake through the entrails of many an old good author with a violation worse than any could be offered to his tomb. [303]

> Thine own begotten, breaking violent way
> Tore through my entrails . . .
>
> Forth issued . . .
>
> Engendering with me, of that rape begot
> These yelling monsters . . .
> [2:782-83,786,794-95]

Considering how different the context, it is astounding how much the phrasing is the same: "engendering"—"engendering"; "brought forth"—"forth issued"; "rake through the entrails"—"tore through my entrails"; "violation"—"violent." Needless to say, to violate a tomb is not to violate a womb, and "entrails" has a different reference in the prose, suggesting the priest-augur poring over intestines for signs and also the hangman "drawing," disemboweling, his victim. But, after all, it is the author, rather than his tomb, that is being violated, and "entrails" is as close as Milton can get to *womb,* in view of his experience that authors are invariably male (cf. "Lycidas" 19-21). As close as he can get in one sentence, that is; the paragraph becomes hermaphroditic:

> Till then books were ever as freely admitted into the world as any other birth; the issue of the brain was no more stifled than the issue of the womb: no envious Juno sat cross-legged over the nativity of any man's intellectual offspring; but if it proved a

monster, who denies but that it was justly burnt, or sunk into the sea? [305; compare "the birth . . . of books," 322.]

To quote Blake's *Jerusalem* (76), "These are the Female Males." Furthermore, despairing Adam, when he longs for death, makes a womb-tomb equation, "how glad would lay me down/As in my mother's lap" (10:777-78). St. Sigmund will go wild here, and the latest critic will contend that "mould" (10:744) is a pun.[37]

As for entrails-womb, a bit of unnatural natural history makes a connection. *Of Reformation* alluded to this: "Let not the obstinacy of our half-obedience and will-worship bring forth that viper of sedition that for these four-score years hath been breeding to eat through the entrails of our peace; but let her cast her abortive spawn without the danger of this travailling and throbbing kingdom" (*Works,* III, 77). The editors are silent, but Sir Thomas Browne explains: "That the young vipers force their way through the bowels of their dam, or that the female viper in the act of generation bites off the head of the male, in revenge whereof the young ones eat through the womb and belly of the female, is a very ancient tradition." Thus, as again the editors do not tell us, in tearing through his dam's entrails at birth Death was being viperous, and his offspring still are: "hourly conceived/And hourly born, with sorrow infinite/To me; for when they list, into the womb/That bred them they return, and howl and gnaw/My bowels, their repast" (2:796-800; cf. 656-59).[38]

The word "monster" in the "Juno . . . cross-legged" sentence renews the whole "engendering" parallel. The late Kester Svendsen[39] remarked, "The motifs of miscegenation, hermaphroditism, and disnatured conception occur in the prose and have their counterpart in the epic." One recalls that "loathèd Melancholy" was "of Cerberus and blackest Midnight born" ("L'Allegro" 1-2)—a promising start for a hideous series. Is it inquiring too curiously to ask who, in the union of the Council of Trent and the Spanish Inquisition, is the female? Presumably the latter, on the basis of a prior phrase that also sounds hell-whelpish: "This project of licencing crept out of the Inquisition" (299). And was not the copulation monstrous and bound to produce monstrous offspring, for two reasons: on account of incest and on account of a generation gap? Certainly it is Milton's point that the Council of Trent and the Spanish Inquisition are closely related. But the former was born in 1545, while the latter dates from 1478,[40] when Ferdinand and Isabella obtained papal approval for it. Thus the female is sixty-seven years older than her lover, a disgusting and eugenically unpromising situation, as indeed incest has always been thought to be. Michael Lieb[41] comments on the *Paradise Lost* passage: "With the stress upon inbreeding and offspring among the three diabolic figures, we are presented with the primitive idea that inbreeding is related to deformed, unhealthy, indeed, monstrous offspring." The monstrous offspring in *Areopagitica,* Catalogues of Forbidden Books and Indexes of Censored Books, tear and torment entrails-wombs with the pertinacity of Sin's hellhounds.

They are *expurging* Indexes, a more emphatic form of purging. No good will issue from that operation, from those entrails. It is creation in reverse—and how well the unflinching Dante would have understood it! Nor does Milton dodge the implication, in this same paragraph: "I fear their next design will be to get into their custody the licencing of that which they say Claudius intended, but went not through with" (304). Milton's marginal note gives, in the decency of Latin, a reference to flatulence. All this, too, looks forward (or backward) to what Lieb, in his provocative book *The Dialectics of Creation: Patterns of Birth and Regeneration in "Paradise Lost,"* analyzes as the anality of Hell. We have, before we ever reach the unholy Trinity, the "fueled entrails" "of thundering Etna" (1:233ff.), on which Lieb expatiates, "The hill is torn forcibly because of a 'subterranean wind,' and Etna erupts because its 'combustible' and 'fewel'd entrails' undergo a process of pregnancy and birth: the 'entrails,' whose normal function is excretory, now perform a generative function in their conceiving of fire. The combustible birth is certainly of an anal nature, for the eruption of the entrails 'leave[s] a singed bottom all involv'd/With stench and smoak.' "[42] Embarrassingly plain is the *analogy* of the infernal cannon, "whose roar/ Emboweled with outrageous noise the air,/And all her entrails tore, disgorging foul/Their devilish glut" (6:586-89). "Tore through my entrails" (2:783)—"And all her entrails tore" (6:588): birth has been connected with the digestive system, as in folklore and in psychoanalysis and in *Areopagitica* (always remembering that the word proceeds from the mouth).

In his *Animadversions,* 1641, Milton had already grumbled over "monkish prohibitions and expurgatorious Indexes" (*Works,* III, 112). The date for the birth of the monstrous progeny of his 1644 sentence can be given as 1559, when the Index Librorum Prohibitorum and the Index Expurgatorius were approved by the Council of Trent (that is, recognized by the father). Some further historical remarks are worth making. The next sentence in *Areopagitica* reads: "Nor did they stay in matters heretical, but any subject that was not to their palate they either condemned in a prohibition, or had it straight into the new purgatory of an Index" (303). One of Milton's favorite authors was thus banned, as Jebb[43] did not know when he recorded the following: "The first Italian index, containing about 70 books, was printed by Giovanni della Casa, an intimate friend of [Cardinal] Caraffa, at Venice. More complete catalogues appeared in 1552 at Florence and in 1554 at Milan. In 1559 a catalogue was printed at Rome [Caraffa having become Pope Paul IV] in the form which long remained the model: it included the writings of Cardinals, and Casa's own poems." In December 1629 Milton bought (for ten pence) a copy of the 1563 Venice edition of della Casa's poems,[44] which survives, and which greatly influenced his own English and Italian sonnets.[45] Thus particular annoyance over the condemnation of "an old good author" much to his "palate" may have sharpened his reference. Della Casa had died three years before, in 1556;

to be put on the Index was "a violation worse than any could be offered to his tomb."

Yet there is the irony that the Italian poet had cooperated in printing a Catalogue of Prohibited Books, even as Milton served briefly as a licencer of a newsletter[46] under the Commonwealth. The key sentence of 1644 happens to be prophetic of a good deal of Milton's future besides *Paradise Lost.* Books of his suffered the purgatory—"the fire and the executioner" (353)—of being publicly burned by the common executioner in France before the Restoration and in England after.[47] Indeed Herbert Palmer in a sermon before Parliament had already singled out *The Doctrine and Discipline of Divorce* as "deserving to be burnt."[48] On 23 November 1694, as if timed for the exact fiftieth anniversary of *Areopagitica,* Milton's Letters of State were put on the Roman Catholic Index Librorum Prohibitorum. Paolo Rolli's translation of *Paradise Lost* followed in 1732.[49] As for "violation . . . to his tomb," that came to him, too, not so soon as to Cromwell, Bradshaw, and Ireton, but in 1790. A contemporary narrative of that act of desecration by morbid curiosity-seekers and mercenary souvenir-hunters echoes Milton's key word in referring to "the sole atonement, which can now be made, to the violated rights of the dead."[50]

The two Adam passages in *Areopagitica* have often been quoted, but little commented on. The first has the author's characteristic mix of Christian and pagan story:

> Good and evil we know in the field of this world grow up together almost inseparably; and the knowledge of good is so involved and interwoven with the knowledge of evil, and in so many cunning resemblances hardly to be discerned, that those confused seeds which were imposed on Psyche as an incessant labor to cull out and sort asunder, were not more intermixed. It was from out the rind of one apple tasted that the knowledge of good and evil, as two twins cleaving together, leaped forth into the world. And perhaps this is that doom which Adam fell into of knowing good and evil, that is to say, of knowing good by evil. [311-12]

The student of Milton's imagery notes, "He is fond of the

metaphor of twins, which he uses eight times, although it seems to have no special psychological significance."[51] It is probably not in the same class with his monster imagery, which may be seen as part of what John Carey[52] decides is "the uneasiness Milton feels on the subject of fecundity." Carey's earlier chapter on the prose infers: "The images draw on organic processes almost exclusively for the purpose of conveying disgust. There is no complementary strain of healthful bodily functions."[53] Those twins are not both good, and a reference in *The Reason of Church Government* to "a certain monstrous haste of pregnancy" (*Works,* III, 211) is a reminder—we have been looking at others—that there are cells that should not multiply.

Editors should put beside the last sentence in the quoted paragraph the same statement in *De Doctrina Christiana:* "It was called the tree of knowledge of good and evil from the event; for since Adam tasted it, we not only know evil, but we know good only by means of evil." ". . . Sed ne bonum quidem nisi per malum"[54]—a pun, since "malum" is also Latin for *apple*. The Adam of *Paradise Lost* breaks out with greater pessimism: "Since our eyes/Opened we find indeed, and find we know/Both good and evil, Good lost and evil got,/Bad fruit of knowledge" (9:1070-73).

The *Areopagitica* sentence that mentions the apple dangles before us a twofold meaning. First, we are put in mind of Eve by the very absence of mention of her. The apple has been divided in "two," split into two hemispheres for the loss of one world: Eve ate the first half. The couple—"cleaving" having simultaneously the opposite meanings of separate and together—are under "doom." The second meaning is that the apple has a worm in it, evil. Satan is the serpent called "worm" in *Paradise Lost* (9:1068). We ought then to remember the early appearance of "rind" in the poem, involving the Devil as Leviathan, whom "The pilot of some small night-foundered skiff,/Deeming some island, oft, as seamen tell,/With fixèd anchor in his scaly rind/Moors by his side" (1:204-7).

Finally, to move up to the first sentence, "Good and evil we know in the field of this world grow up together almost inseparably," we seem to have an echo of a statement by St. Ambrose[55] that God "has likewise planted within us a seed-plot of the knowledge of good and evil." Following Philo Judaeus, Ambrose allegorized Eden as "in our highest part, thick set with the growth of many opinions." "In our highest part"—i.e., the soul: this would have set Milton to thinking of Psyche! He has his Apuleian fairy tale, and he has his psychomachy.

The other Adam passage also has to do with the Tree of Knowledge:

Many there be that complain of divine providence for suffering Adam to transgress. Foolish tongues! when God gave him reason, he gave him freedom to choose, for reason is but choosing; he had been else a mere artificial Adam, such an Adam as he is in the motions. We ourselves esteem not of that obedience, or love, or gift, which is of force. God therefore left him free, set before him a provoking object, ever almost in his eyes; herein consisted his merit, herein the right of his reward, the praise of his abstinence. [319]

"Many there be that complain"—Milton has foreseen William Empson and a myriad other of his and God's critics. The contemptuous allusion to "motions" may inform us that the poet has given up any thought of doing a medieval mystery. As Merritt Hughes says in his introduction to *Paradise Lost*,[56] "In puppet shows or 'motions' that drama still survived in Milton's youth, and a capital criticism of its main weakness is implied in Milton's sneer in *Areopagitica* at its failure to make Adam anything but a pawn in a game between God and the Devil."

The *De Doctrina Christiana* betrays what trouble this Christian had making a clean-cut decision with reference to the Tree of Knowledge. Was it just a symbol of obedience, or did it possess, as strongly suggested by the original story (or stories), some magic power? As justifier of God's ways, Milton gives the first interpretation early in his chapter 10

(Book 1): "It was necessary that something should be forbidden or commanded as a test of fidelity, and that an act in its own nature indifferent, in order that man's obedience might be thereby manifested."[57] Thus, as *Areopagitica* so vividly has it, there was "set before him a provoking object." It is to be understood that "the tree of knowledge of good and evil was not a sacrament, as it is generally called; for a sacrament is a thing to be used, not abstained from: but a pledge, as it were, and memorial of obedience."[58] But such insistence is at odds with the allusion in chapter 11 to "the penalty incurred by the violation of things sacred (and such was the tree of knowledge of good and evil)."[59] Grierson[60] uses *this* passage against Milton. "It is a little strange to hear Milton speaking of the tree as a holy thing, in view of his general refusal to recognise holiness in things at all. Is he not here confounding the holiness of principles, of justice, etc. and the sacredness of tabus, the breach of which entails mischief on good and bad alike?" (Basil Willey and B. Rajan also spoke of taboos.[61]) A fuller and fairer account would not pass over chapter 10 and *Areopagitica*. But Milton, who liked to have his cake and eat it too, ultimately fudged it, gave a taste of both interpretations by turning the apple into an intoxicant, as if it were, at the least, hard cider.

The which may remind us that Eve has again returned as a provoking object herself, holding forth the fruit that her spouse, "Against his better knowledge, not deceived,/But fondly overcome with female charm" (9:998-99), chooses not to resist.

Adam knew what he was doing, as Eve did not. "Reason is but choosing"—"Reason also is choice" (3:108) as God explained at length (3:95-128). Aristotle has a word for it that *Of Education* had employed: "By this time, years and good general precepts will have furnished them more distinctly with that act of reason which in ethics is called *proairesis:* that they may with some judgment contemplate upon moral good and evil" (*Works,* IV, 284). Eve would not have been a seemly mention in *Areopagitica,* since Milton wants to keep his discussion on the highest level of right reason, which the Chain of Being showed was male, even as books are male births and none of the Lords and Commons is a woman. (Also, he was smarting from Palmer's attack before Parliament on his "wicked book" on divorce.[62]) Eve comes revengefully back by presenting her husband with the arguments of *Areopagitica* (which the Serpent will also use to her). The prose had been: "If every action which is good or evil to man at ripe years were to be under pittance, and prescription, and compulsion, what were virtue but a name?" (319) The verse is, "And what is faith, love, virtue, unassayed?" (9:335)

The all-too-common assertion that Milton has ceased to believe what he once preached receives its prime answer in the difference in situation between fallen and unfallen man. But another answer is to point out that the *Speech . . . for the Liberty of Unlicenced Printing* does have boundaries, as indeed the phrase "at ripe years" suggests. There is the idea of tutelage, of what Warner Rice[63] calls "a judicious censorship," which is part of Milton's conception that some books in some hands may work mischief. "The rest, as children and childish men . . . well may be exhorted to forbear, but hindered forcibly they cannot be" (315). When Eve, though still sinless, began to reason like a child,[64] Adam sought to impose a judicious censorship on her, but consistent with *Areopagitica,* he did not tie her up. Still, she should not have bound *him:* "Her gifts/Were such as under government well seemed,/Unseemly to bear rule, which was thy part" (10:153-55). Reason did not govern choice or will. "Understanding ruled not" (9:1127).[65]

The two Adam passages prove that Milton had the fall of man on his mind. But then, so do his four outlines for a tragedy. However, what was uniformly missing from the planned *sacre rappresentazione* was the central scene of *Paradise Lost*—the seduction of Adam and Eve. There was, for the play, the problem of nudity or costume (even as Dryden's *The State of Innocence and Fall of Man* was never produced). There was the problem of the speaking Serpent. But the Fall of Man reverberates through *Areopagitica* as it will through *Paradise Lost*. It is a fair guess that, with the theaters closed, Milton had turned his thoughts towards transforming his drama into an epic.

In what way did *Areopagitica* look back on the once planned Arthuriad, last heard of in "Epitaphium Damonis" (circa 1640)? Tillyard[66] quotes the latter portion of the pamphlet that bursts with patriotic fervor: "Lords and Commons of England, consider what nation it is whereof ye are, and whereof ye are the governors . . ." (339). And "Methinks I see in my mind a noble and puissant nation rousing herself like a strong man after sleep, and shaking her invincible locks . . ." (344). But the latter analogy is with Samson and had, indeed, been used in *The Reason of Church Government* (*Works,* III, 276). An Arthuriad would be a national epic that his country would have to deserve. The poet's destiny was tied to that of England.[67] "There be pens and heads there, sitting by their studious lamps, musing, searching, revolving new notions and ideas wherewith to present, as with their homage and their fealty, the approaching reformation" (341). He would eventually sever the patriotic bond in disillusionment and produce a more universal poem. As Tillyard[68] comments, already "in *Areopagitica* beneath the excitement of hope there can be detected the whisper of doubt."

Tillyard's only other citation is more specific, but also more doubtful. "I cannot praise a fugitive and cloistered virtue, unexercised and unbreathed, that never sallies out and sees her adversary, but slinks out of the race, where that immortal garland is to be run for, not without dust and heat" (311). For Tillyard this was more aggressive because, using the Bohn edition, he read "sees her adversary" as "seeks her adversary."[69] However, despite the immediately prior reference to "true wayfaring Christian" corrected to "true warfaring Christian," we seem to have in this sentence, rather than knightly warfare, a race, classical, after the fashion of the Olympic games or Homer and Virgil. (At 9:31ff there is the same sequence of "battle" followed by "races and games.") The only dubious expression is "sallies out." Unless we have mixed metaphors,[70] it means "venture forth" (from the cloister), with perhaps some of the athletic "leap" residue of *salio*. Indeed in the famous footrace in *Aeneid* 5:321ff there is the competitor who happens to be named Salius: Nisus cuts Salius out of the race by blocking him, enabling Euryalus to win. For battle we can do better with William Walwyn, even, who is not suspected of an Arthuriad: "that so errour may discover its foulnesse, and truth become more glorious by a victorious conquest after a fight in open field: they shun the battell that doubt their strength."[71] Surely the Civil War was enough to inspire martial language.

It is surprising that Tillyard did not rather quote:

> When a man hath been laboring the hardest labor in the deep mines of knowledge, hath furnished out his findings in all their equipage, drawn forth his reasons as it were a battle ranged, scattered and defeated all objections in his way, calls out his adversary into the plain, offers him the advantage of wind and sun, if he please; only that he may try the matter by dint of argument, for his opponents then to skulk, to lay ambushments, to keep a narrow bridge of licencing where the challenger should pass, though it be valor enough in souldiership, is but weakness and cowardice in the wars of truth. [347-48]

"Pale trembling coward, there I throw my gage!" (*Richard II* I.i.69) The rhetoric is torn between two worlds—the modern one of "shouldiership" (original spelling), of sneaky and unfair tactics—Prince Rupert's ambushes and King Charles's clever retreats—and the bygone chivalry of open, forthright, individual challenge and combat, the honorable test of strength. Cromwell had begun to look like a knight, while Essex and Manchester acted as if they were definitely trying to avoid victory.

The next year the publisher of Milton's minor poems was to link him and Spenser, and Tillyard's later essay on "Milton and the Epic" sees *The Faerie Queene* as an inevitable influence on any Arthuriad,[72] though not for allegory. Thus any Spenserian, or possibly Spenserian, allusion is suspect, beginning with the naming of him, that "better teacher than Scotus or Aquinas" (311), and Sir Guyon. We look, then, at "the champions of Truth" (336) and think of Book I, Una and the Red Cross Knight[73] and the more effective Prince Arthur. We wonder if a missing episode is being longed for in "Let her and Falsehood grapple; who ever knew Truth put to the worse in a free and open encounter?" (347). Are we to picture Una and Duessa wrestling?[74] Duessa, who presumes to call herself Fidessa? Is this in part another swipe at the Roman Catholic church, the superstitious dragon that this champion of Truth is always ready for another hack at, right up to *Of True Religion,* 1673? "I mean not tolerated popery, and open superstition" (349). Granted that in general and outside allegory "Milton has as little sympathy for the woman-warrior—the *donna guerriera* and the *femme forte*—as for female sovereignty. Both violate the order of nature and female decorum."[75] It was through Spenser that we saw "simple Truth subdue avenging wrong"—in the episode of Una's lion (1:3:6:5). Milton has so many figurative excursions, one-sentence allegories. But female knights are rare enough, except in *The Faerie Queene.* Even here, though, Hughes[76] would have us see the epic of salvation: "All the faith in Truth's power to crush Falsehood in any open encounter that Milton poured into *Areopagitica* is symbolized in the all-seeing eyes of the victorious Son's chariot."[77]

It does not add up to much, that inchoate never-born Arthuriad, compared to those hooked atoms (as the author of *The Road to Xanadu* would have called them) that eventually became manifest in *Paradise Lost.*

Notes

1 E. M. W. Tillyard, *Milton* (New York, 1967), pp. 163ff; Sir H. J. C. Grierson, *Milton and Wordsworth* (Cambridge, 1937), pp. 71-72; F. E. Hutchinson, *Milton and the English Mind* (London, 1946), p. 84. Cf. Lawrence A. Sasek, "Milton's Patriotic Epic," HLQ, 20 (1956), 1-14.

2 William Haller, *The Rise of Puritanism* (New York, 1938), p. 318.

3 Arthur E. Barker, *Milton and the Puritan Dilemma* (Toronto, 1942), p. 15.

4 *Chariot of Wrath* (London, 1942), pp. 97-98.

5 Don M. Wolfe and William Alfred, p. 519 of *Complete Prose Works of John Milton,* I (New Haven, 1953).

6 *Milton* (Oxford, 1968), II, 911-17.

7 *Of Education,* Columbia *Works,* IV, 286.

8 John S. Diekhoff, *Milton's "Paradise Lost": A Commentary on the Argument* (New York, reprint edition, 1958), p. 1.

9 Ed. *Tracts on Liberty in the Puritan Revolution, 1638-1647* (New York, 1934), I, 75. Compare the same author's *Liberty and Reformation in the Puritan Revolution* (New York, 1955), p. 184: "a poet's expression of the excitement of a people." Similar remarks can be found, early and late: e.g., "Milton's *Areopagitica* is prose, but it is the prose of a poet, gorgeous in imagery, and full of noble music" (W. E. A. Axon in *Milton Memorial Lectures,* ed. Percy W. Ames [London, 1909], p. 45). "In his immortal half-poetic prose essay . . . " (Charles G. Osgood, *Poetry as a Means of Grace* [Princeton, 1941], p. 41). "Rightly and inevitably we consider Milton's prose as a poetic performance" (Michael S. Davis, ed., *"Areopagitica" and "Of Education"* [New York, 1963], p. 12). Parker's characterization was "prose hymn of hope" (*Milton,* p. 275).

10 Wolfe, *Milton in the Puritan Revolution* (New York, 1941), p. 124.

11 Parker, p. 85.

12 Tillyard, p. 167; cf. pp. 133-34, 136-37.

13 See J. Horrell, "Milton, Limbo, and Suicide," *RES,*

18 (1942), 413-27.

14 Edward Phillips in Darbishire, pp. 72-73.

15 Ed. *Areopagitica* (London), p. 2.

16 "The bottomless pit" is also in *Of Reformation, Works,* III, 76 (cf. *Tenure of Kings,* V, 59), as is "beatific vision," 79. "Mortal things" makes a reappearance in *Paradise Regained* 4:318.

17 Tillyard, p. 137.

18 First expressed in the third prolusion: "Sed nec iisdem, quibus orbis, limitibus contineri et circumscribi se patiatur vestra mens, sed . . . divagetur" (*Works,* XII, 170).

19 Isabel MacCaffrey, *"Paradise Lost" as "Myth"* (Cambridge, Mass., 1959), finds "the word *wander* . . . a key word" in the epic, p. 188, having "almost always a pejorative, or melancholy connotation," but Stanley Fish well argues against that view as exaggerated, *Surprised by Sin: The Reader in "Paradise Lost"* (London, 1967), pp. 130ff. Cf. William G. Riggs, *The Christian Poet in "Paradise Lost"* (Berkeley, 1972), pp. 26-31.

20 See Harry F. Robins, *If This Be Heresy: A Study of Milton and Origen* (Urbana, 1963), pp. 75ff; Denis Saurat, *Milton et le matérialisme chrétien en Angleterre* (Paris 1928).

21 He fails for some commentators. "One obvious rhetorical device he employed was none too subtle flattery" (J. Max Patrick, ed., *The Prose of John Milton* [New York 1967], p. 251). "His specious flattery" (Rose Macaulay, *Milton* [London, 1957], p. 90). "He humbles himself to management and the seasonings of flattery" (Sir Walter Raleigh, *Milton* [London, 1900], p. 56).

22 Fish, p. 15.

23 Wilbur E. Gilman must be given credit for at least mentioning this, in a 3-line footnote, p. 23 of *Milton's Rhetoric: Studies in his Defense of Liberty* (Columbia, Missouri, 1939), followed twenty years later by seven lines in the first footnote of the Yale editor. Since 1929 a much-used textbook has said noncommittally, "For another famous address in connection with the Areopagus (Mars' Hill), see St. Paul's speech, Acts 17" (Robert P. T. Coffin and Alexander M. Witherspoon, *A Book of Seventeenth-Century Prose* [New York], p. 408; same footnote in the latest revision by Wither-

spoon and Frank J. Warnke, *Seventeenth-Century Prose and Poetry* [1963], p. 395).

24 Douglas Bush, *English Literature in the Earlier Seventeenth Century* (1st ed., Oxford, 1945), p. 330.

25 According to the marginal note in the King James Bible. *The Oxford Dictionary of the Christian Church,* ed. F. L. Cross (London, 1958), p. 80, s.v. *Areopagus,* summarizes: "It is not entirely clear whether, when St. Paul was brought to the Areopagus to explain his 'new teaching' (Acts 17:19), it was before the official court or whether the place was merely chosen as convenient for a meeting. The language of Acts suggests the latter view, though a marginal note in some MSS indicates the other alternative, which was that adopted by St. Chrysostom."

26 Ed. *Areopagitica* (Cambridge, 1918), p. xxiii.

27 Presentation to Rouse, *Works,* XVIII, 270; *Defensio Secunda, Works,* VIII, 134.

28 For references and citations see Yale *Prose* (New Haven), II (1959), 507, 508, 512, 515, 549, 554, 561, 563, 564, 565, 566. Note especially "this Christian liberty which *Paul* so often boasts of" (563) (Columbia *Works,* IV, 348).

29 The application of this phrase, appearing five times in his poetry, degenerates like Lucifer: "Arcades" 2; "Lycidas" 74; *Paradise Lost* 1:665; 4:818; 10:453. One could discourse on what I should call Milton's siege mentality, which deepened in blindness and in political defeat. Angus Fletcher's chapter "The Bound Man" is suggestive: *The Transcendental Masque: An Essay on Milton's "Comus"* (Ithaca, 1971), pp. 195ff.

30 *Milton,* I, 145.

31 VIII, 60. But he has courage and is adept with the sword, like King Edgar, who well knew how to answer the insult "such a little dapper man." *History of Britain, Works,* X, 244.

32 In Darbishire, pp. 32, 3.

33 TLS, 3 November 1932, p. 815; James Holly Hanford, *John Milton, Englishman* (New York, 1949), p. 65; and in some editions of Hanford's *A Milton Handbook* (New York), e.g., 1939, p. 160, but the subject has been dropped in the latest (fifth) edition done with James G. Taaffe, 1970.

34 *Works,* VIII, 60.

35 From 2 Corinthians 12:9. Parker, I, 389.

36 Patrick in his edition mistakenly has "expurgating," p. 279.

37 Apropos of Mother and Mother Earth, ch. 11 of *Eikonoklastes* has a sentence beginning, "And if it hath been anciently interpreted the presaging sign of a future tyrant . . . to dream of copulation with his mother" (*Works,* V, 186). "Robert Allott, *Wits Theater of the Little World* (1599), supplies an explanation of the cryptic allusion: 'Caesar dreamed, that hee lay with his mother, which the Sooth-sayers interpreting, the earth to bee his mother, sayde, That hee should bee conquerour of the world' " (Kester Svendsen, *Milton and Science* [Cambridge, Mass., 1956], p. 189). The Talmud found such a dream "signified the attainment of the highest degree of wisdom." See J. E. Cirlot, *A Dictionary of Symbols* (New York, 1962), p. xlvii. Relevant is Arnold Toynbee's distillation of Frazer:

> . . . The image of the seed that dies and is buried in the womb of Mother Earth and then rises again in next year's crop or in the next generation of a human family. The image went into action in the worship of the sorrowing mother or wife and her suffering son or husband who has met a violent death and achieved a glorious resurrection. This religion radiated out of the Land of Sumer to the ends of the Earth. The Sumerian goddess Inanna (better known under her Akkadian name Ishtar) and her consort Tammuz reappear in Egypt as Isis and Osiris, in Canaan as Astarte and Adonis, in the Hittite World as Cybele and Attis, and in distant Scandinavia as Nana and Balder—the goddess here still bearing her original Sumerian name, while the god, in Scandinavia as in Canaan, becomes an anonymous 'Our Lord.'
>
> *Hellenism* (New York, 1959), p. 12

So the Isis and Osiris paragraph (*Areopagitica* 338) is another augur of things to come. As for the author's ambivalence of sex, like that of the angels, "When a poet speaks of the *internal* spirit which shapes the poem, he is apt to drop the traditional appeal to female Muses and think of himself as in a feminine, or at least receptive, relation to some god or lord, whether Apollo, Dionysus, Eros, Christ, or (as in Milton) the Holy Spirit" (Northrop Frye, *Anatomy of Criticism* [New York, 1967], p. 98). With typical bravado Nietzsche put it, "I know both sides, for I am both sides" (first paragraph of "Why I Am So Wise," *Ecce Homo: The Philosophy of Nietzsche* [New York, Modern Library], p. 817). Cf. the chapter on "Creation," passim, in W. B. C. Watkins, *An Anatomy of Milton's Verse* (Baton Rouge, 1955); John T. Shawcross, "The Metaphor of Inspiration in *Paradise Lost,*" pp. 75-85 of Amadeus P. Fiore, ed., *Th'Upright Heart and Pure* (Pittsburgh, 1967); Michael Lieb, *The Dialectics of Creation* (Amherst, 1970), p. 44.

38 The "thousand yong ones" of Spenser's Error return "into her mouth" (*The Faerie Queene* 1:1:15), as Browne maintained was observable of vipers: "For the young one supposed to break through the belly of the Dam, will upon any fright for protection run into it; for then the old one receives them in at her mouth, which way the fright being past, they will return again, which is a peculiar way of refuge; and although it seem strange is avowed by frequent experience and undeniable testimony." Milton, thinking more of Scylla, details a still more "peculiar way of refuge." Both quotations from Browne come, needless to say, from the *Pseudodoxia Epidemica* (Third Book, ch. 16 *Works,* ed. G. Keynes [London, 1928], II, 237, 238).

39 P. 188.

40 E. Sirluck, p. 493, n. 26 of Yale *Prose Works,* II, wrongly states, ". . . In 1478, Torquemada was appointed first Grand Inquisitor." That was not to be until 1483.

41 Pp. 161-62.

42 Ibid., pp. 30-31. Cf. "the first broadside," antipapal cartoon by Martin Luther and Lucas Cranach, *Birth of the Papacy,* woodcut, 1545, reproduced in *Art News,* 70 (1972), p. 51.

43 Ed. *Areopagitica,* p. 76.

44 Parker, I, 61; II, 749-50.

45 The latest discussion is in *A Variorum Commentary on the Poems of John Milton,* I, Italian Poems, ed. J. E. Shaw and A. Bartlett Giamatti (New York, 1970), pp. 371ff.

46 *Mercurius Politicus,* Parker, I, 394.

47 Parker, I, 387-88; 574; cf. 661.

48 Ibid., 263.

49 Ibid., II, 1185.

50 [Philip Neve], *A Narrative of the Disinterment of Milton's Coffin in the Parish-Church of St. Giles, Cripplegate, on Wednesday, 4th of August, 1790; and of the Treatment of*

the Corpse During that, and the following day (London, 1790), pp. 32-33. See further French V, 136; Allen W. Read, "The Disinterment of Milton's Remains," *PMLA,* 45 (1930), 1050-68; James G. Nelson, *The Sublime Puritan* (Madison, 1963), pp. 4-5. Happily the strands of hair that occasioned poems from Leigh Hunt and Keats were not those exhumed on this occasion but came from Milton's youngest daughter Deborah to Addison: see French, V, 135.

51 Theodore H. Banks, *Milton's Imagery* (New York, 1950), p. 69.

52 *Milton* (London, 1969), p. 105. The opposite opinion is based more on the poetry. "It was Saurat, I believe, who first pointed out the feeling Milton had for fertility, for exuberant life. It is a simple and very common feeling, but Milton had it with a force quite exceptional even among poets, as if his own teeming brain and soaring temperament were in some intimate way linked with the apparent lavishness of nature in perpetuating the forms of life." Tillyard, *The Miltonic Setting* (London, 1938), p. 69.

53 Ibid., pp. 68-69. Are, then, the twins monstrous? So White, p. 62, found them and compared 12:83-85 and *Eikonoklastes,* ch. 21 (*Works,* V, 254).

54 *Works,* XV, 114.

55 Letter to Sabinus, *Library of Fathers,* XLV, quoted (not in this connection) by J. M. Evans, *"Paradise Lost" and the Genesis Tradition* (Oxford, 1968), p. 74. The Latin is, "Constituit etiam scientiae boni et mali seminarium (8). "Ergo paradisus in principali nostro est, silvescens plurimarum opinionum plantariis" (7). Migne, *Patrologia Latina,* XVI, 1192. I would guess that Ambrose's inspiration may have been the parable of the wheat and the tares, also referred to in *Areopagitica* (349), Matthew 13:24-30; interpreted 36-43. Note especially 38: "The field is the world: the good seed are the children of the kingdom; but the tares are the children of the wicked one." Saurat, *Milton Man and Thinker* (New York, 1925), p. 292, quoted the *Zohar*: "Had not the Holy One (Blessed be He) created the spirit of good and the spirit of evil, man could have had neither merit nor demerit; that is the reason why God created him a mixture of the two spirits." Apropos of Milton's optimism, note, since his title page quotes Euripides' *The Suppliants,* Theseus's dictum: "For there are who say, there is more bad than good in human nature, to the

which I hold a contrary view, that good o'er bad predominates in man, for if it were not so, we should not exist" (tr. E. P. Coleridge, p. 925 of *The Complete Greek Drama,* ed. W. J. Oates and Eugene O'Neill, Jr. [New York, 1938], I). (Incidentally, if Milton had continued his quotation from the play, lines 442ff, he would have proclaimed himself an antimonarchist: "Again, where the people are absolute rulers of the land, they rejoice in having a reserve of youthful citizens, while a king counts this a hostile element, and strives to slay the leading men, all such as he deems discreet, for he feareth for his power" [Oates and O'Neill, ibid., 931].)

56 Ed. *Complete Poetry and Major Prose* (New York, 1957), p. 175.

57 *Works,* XV, 113-15.

58 Ibid., 115.

59 Ibid., 185. The rationale seems to be that Milton wanted to add "sacrilege" to the heap of crimes Adam and Eve were guilty of, 181-83.

60 Pp. 96-97.

61 Willey, *The Seventeenth Century Background* (London, 1934), pp. 250-51. B. Rajan, *"Paradise Lost" and the Seventeenth Century Reader* (London, 1947), p. 45: "the unintelligible taboo against eating the fruit." See M. Y. Hughes, "Beyond Disobedience, *Approaches to "Paradise Lost,"* ed. C. A. Patrides (London, 1968), pp. 181-98.

62 Compare Harold J. Laski's comment, "The *Areopagitica* is the sublimation of a Milton who resents the criticism of his marriage-theories." P. 171 in Hermon Ould, ed., *Freedom of Expression* (London, 1945).

63 "A Note on *Areopagitica," JEGP,* 40 (1941), 478. Compare footnote in Hanford-Taaffe, *Handbook,* p. 81: "In *The Reason of Church Government* [*Works,* III, 239] . . . Milton did argue that the magistrates exercise their power to prevent young men from being influenced by 'libidinous and ignorant Poetasters.' "

64 ". . . We are told that Eve has suddenly taken it into her head to go and do her pruning by herself. Adam makes a long speech, in impeccable blank verse, pointing out that, as they are about to be assailed by a clever and ruthless enemy, it might be better for them to stay together and not separate. Eve says that that is very true, and that she would like to go

off and prune by herself. Adam makes another long speech, in equally impeccable blank verse, making the same point with elaborations. Eve says that all that is very true, and that she will now go off and prune by herself" (Northrop Frye, *The Return of Eden* [Toronto, 1965], p. 67). Since the Women's Liberation movement there have appeared three articles insisting on Eve's responsibility for her actions: Diane K. McColley, "Free Will and Obedience in the Separation Scene in *Paradise Lost,*" *SEL,* 12 (1972), 103-20; Elaine B. Safer, " 'Sufficient To Have Stood': Eve's Responsibility in Book IX," *MQ,* 6 (1972), 10-14; Stella P. Revard, "Eve and the Doctrine of Responsibility in *Paradise Lost,*" *PMLA,* 88, (1973), 69-78.

65 On the theological background, see A. B. Chambers, "The Falls of Adam and Eve in *Paradise Lost,*" pp. 118-30 in Thomas Kranidas, ed., *New Essays on "Paradise Lost"* (Berkeley, 1969).

66 Pp. 134-35.

67 See Joan Webber, *The Eloquent "I": Style and Self in Seventeenth-Century Prose* (Madison, 1968), pp. 188ff.

68 P. 135.

69 Elsewhere I have argued that this may have been the reading Milton intended. *Yet Once More: Verbal and Psychological Pattern in Milton* (New York, 1953; reprinted 1969), p. 149. Stefan Grotz (in a master's essay written at the University of California, Berkeley, 1963, "Milton: A Study of Psychological Tension") has pointed to the parallel with Elegia VII, 57: "Haec ego non fugi spectacula grata severus."

70 "Milton normally favors a simple metaphor or simile." Alan F. Price, "Incidental Imagery in *Areopagitica,*" *MP,* 49 (1952), 222. Whether "wayfaring" be cast out or not, it should be noticed that *Areopagitica* has, besides "wars of Truth" (348), "ways of Truth" (344): the which supplies a title for Ruth M. Kivette's article voting for "wayfaring," "The Ways and Wars of Truth," *Milton Quarterly,* 6 (1972), 81-86.

71 Quoted in the introduction to Yale *Prose Works,* II, 87, from *The Compassionate Samaritane* (London, 1644), pp. 55-56. This plea for religious toleration had come out in June or July. Walwyn in another tract and others are instanced by Hughes, "Milton as a Revolutionary," *Ten Perspectives on Milton* (New Haven, 1965), pp. 262-63.

72 "I conclude that Milton meant to use Spenser as Tasso had used Ariosto. He would adopt the total historical and patriotic material of Spenser and recast it in the neo-classic form of Tasso" (*The Miltonic Setting,* p. 192). For the "narrow bridge" passage John W. Hales, ed., *Areopagitica* (Oxford, 1904), p. 146, quotes *The Faerie Queene* 5:2:4. On Milton's attitude in his three long poems, see George Williamson, "Milton the Anti-Romantic," *Milton and Others* (Chicago, 1970), pp. 11-25. We have the paradox of "an heroic poet who denounced the central values of ancient heroic poetry" (J. H. Summers, "Milton and the Cult of Conformity" [1956], reprinted in *Milton: Modern Judgements,* ed. A. Rudrum [London, 1968], p. 32).

73 For a different association, see Mother M. Christopher Pecheux, "Spenser's Red Cross and Milton's Adam," *ELN,* 6 (1969), 246-51.

74 A skill that is part of being a good warrior, as *Of Education* made explicit: "They must be also practised in all the locks and grips of wrestling, wherein Englishmen were wont to excel, as need may often be in fight to tug, to grapple, and to close" (*Works,* IV, 288). *The Reason of Church Government* made "the fierce encounter of Truth and Falsehood together" "so violent a jousting" (III, 224).

75 John M. Steadman, *Milton and the Renaissance Hero* (Oxford, 1967), p. 126. Boadicea is a case in point. See my "Milton's Attitude towards Women in the *History of Britain,*" *PMLA,* 62 (1947), 977-83.

76 Ed. *Complete Poems and Major Prose* (New York, 1957), p. 178.

77 Compare "kills reason itself, kills the image of God, as it were in the eye" (298) with "One Spirit in them ruled, and every eye / Glared lightning" (6:848-49). Four years after *Areopagitica* Richard Crashaw published "In the Glorious Epiphanie of Our Lord God, A Hymn. Sung as by the Three Kings," of which lines 13-14 read: "The EAST is come / To seek her self in thy sweet Eyes" (*Complete Poetry,* ed. G. W. Williams [New York, 1970], p. 40). "Grapple" enters Milton's poetry in a significant parallel at the end of *Paradise Regained* (4:567). See the annotations in *Poems,* ed. John Carey and Alastair Fowler (London, 1968), p. 1164. Pascal is supremely relevant: "La Vérité subsiste éternellement et triomphe enfin de ses ennemis, parce qu'elle est éternelle et puissante comme Dieu même" (*Provinciales,* Lettre 12, cited

by E. de Guerle, *Milton, Sa vie et ses oeuvres* [Paris, 1868], pp. 230-31).

THE SATIRIST AND WIT

With the Milton industry being only less than the Shakespeare industry, and the scraping—sometimes the re-scraping—of the bottom of the barrel being heard in numerous parts of the groves of academe, it is surprising there has not been a book on Milton as satirist and wit.[1] The materials are on hand, with annotations, and they are timely. With the tercentenary of Milton's death coming up, one may even experience a nostalgia for a strong trait and talent ordinarily passed over as a weakness about which the less said the better. Milton! thou shouldst be living at this hour, not as a soul dwelling apart but as a fighter in the arena. The age "hath need of thee"—because it needs a satirist. Mary McCarthy, William F. Buckley, Jr., and acid reviews and letters in the *Times Literary Supplement* and the *New York Review of Books* do not quite suffice. Our condition calls for "sharp, but saving words,"[2] but the rumble around us lacks lightning and light. Making angry noises is hardly enough. Loud is not clear. Our would-be saviors offer chants in unison, or mumble, or irrational ramble, "rhetoric" without style, name-calling as innocent of originality as it is of tradition. In the midst of all the passionate intensity one longs for skill and mind and character.

However, enough of beating our own times, pleasurable though that tends to be; let us rather examine how Milton beat his. Admittedly he composed no formal satires, unless a half-dozen epigrams in Latin or Greek count as such. (E. K. Rand thought that "In Quintum Novembris" came close: "One of the most powerful of his poems . . . but in structure it is an epyllion, a mock-epyllion, rather than satire."[3]) Yet the recent critic who goes so far as to say, "The comic forms expressing satirical and ironic themes, he [Milton] found uncongenial," has to qualify by mentioning in the next sentence the Hobson poems, and complicates the issue by referring later to "the antimasque of grotesque deities" in the Nativity Ode and the section of "demonic parody" in *Comus*.[4] The 1966 Yale Milton is also, as we shall see, initially beset with contradictions, from failure to give Milton as polemicist his due.

One can agree with Tillyard[5] and Patrick Cruttwell[6] and J. B. Leishman[7] that he was not a "metaphysical" wit, despite a conceit or two in his earliest English poetry. Nor was he a Restoration wit, though Allan Gilbert[8] found the lustful encounter of Adam and Eve on a "shady bank" after the Fall suggestive of "the jocose poems" like those in the *Windsor Drollery*, and though misogynistic phrases from *Samson Agonistes* turn up, with lighter weight, in *Aureng-Zebe*, and Farquhar and Congreve made similar borrowings.[9] Principally, and because of his principles, Milton lived on in the days of Charles II as an anachronism, but he was strangely updated.

If by any chance the word *wit* is used to hint at a sense of humor, the implication is bound to meet with the most vigorous resistance, for does not everybody know, and has not nearly everybody said,[10] that this was one poet utterly lacking in that important quality? Speak of humor in *Paradise Lost*, and what will the knowing reader immediately think of? "No fear lest dinner cool" (5:396)? It is probably no exaggeration to use the word *resent*, as Douglas Bush does: "Some readers, who think Milton should be always solemn, . . . resent this little vegetarian joke."[11] Or there is Belial's jest, after the infernal cannon have bowled the good angels over: "Leader, the terms we sent were terms of weight,/ Of hard contents, and full of force urged home,/ Such as we might perceive amused them all,/ And stumbled many" (6:621-24). These oppugners are no better than "*puny* habitants" (2:367), with a *low* sense of humor.

It may be that it takes a devil today to be "amused" by these puns. (Accused by Filip von Zesen in 1661 of "teuflischen Aberwitz,"[12] Milton had cannonaded Hall in similar fashion: the remonstrant having spoken of "the battery of their paper-pellets," he was answered: "If pellets will not do, your own canons shall be turned against you."[13]) On the other hand it may be that we are too sadly far from unfallen man to share Adam's innocent "mirth" (4:346) on the occasion of the elephant's wreathing "his lithe proboscis" (a deliberately ponderous noun that puts the frisky pachyderm before us). Perhaps this is only for children at circuses.

It could be that it is only we who are solemn. For instance, "Our thin decorum is nervous about admitting the comic to proximity with the official sublime."[14] Therefore we fail to appreciate that "No fear lest dinner cool" is "one of the genuinely *achieved* comic lines in English"—fitting into the "domestic, 'middle-class,' comic" that much of the rest of Book 5 is. The critic who says this is himself funny—"Supply and brilliantly Milton's picture of Adam and Eve in the garden expands and contracts in a kind of systolic decorum of the needs of the subject"—but all by way of reminder that the angelic digestion is also comic and contains a "dazzling conceit"[15]—pun—: "Your bodies may at last turn all to spirit,/ Improved by *tract* of time" (5:497-98, italics added). As for the so often deplored Book 6, Arnold Stein[16] rescued that by analyzing it as an extended metaphor and intentionally ridiculous.

This is one of the problems. When was Milton smiling? The jest in "At a Vacation Exercise" on a fellow student named Rivers was lost for two centuries, recovered between the first edition and the second of volume I of Masson's *Life,* but is still lost to some:[17] for instance Dora Raymond in

1932[18] complained of "an irrelevant address to the rivers of England"; on the other hand this biographer observed (assisted by Warton), "When asked to indite Latin iambics on the Platonic Idea as Aristotle understood it, this disconcerting student produced such absurdities as to qualify his opus for inclusion in a burlesque book of 1715, made up of specimens of unintelligible metaphysics."[19]

Solemn ourselves, we ought to keep questioning, as Tillyard so often did. Is Sonnet 8, "Captain or colonel," "slightly humorous in tone"?[20] Was the poet "making fun of Ellwood when remarking 'pleasantly' that Ellwood had put *Paradise Regained* into his head"?[12] Is the opening of "L'Allegro" a burlesque?[22] Is "or o'er the tiles" (*P.L.* 4:191) "a perfect touch of deliberate comedy"?[23]

When Milton *is* unmistakable, we turn aside. "Our" Milton wrote Prolusio VII, on the blessings of knowledge, but not VI, "Sportive Exercises do not stand in the way of Philosophic Studies." Mrs. Tillyard[24] declined to translate some lines of the latter, which make the same unwholesome reference as the ending of canto 21 of the *Inferno.* (Milton apologized profusely; Dante—Hell was Hell—did not.) The Lady of Christ's was producing the crude humor that was expected. Even the apology was traditional. One old prolusion in manuscript at the university library, Cambridge,[25] begins in English: "Once more welcome as degrees to our inscriptions—in a word you are welcome as you are come. Now why? do not ask me to what, I confess you could not come in a worse time, but such as we have, truly ye have it with a good will. Truly if we had known of your coming and mother had provided something else—but pray set down." Evidently salutatorians have never ceased to struggle, self-consciously, with their obligation to clown.

Leigh Hunt wanted to include in an anthology the splendidly scornful "tailed" sonnet "On the New Forcers of Conscience under the Long Parliament," but was stopped by the Biblical word "whore"—"the widowed whore, Plurality." "As ladies, it is hoped, as well as gentlemen, will read the book, and the sonnet of the indignant poet contains a word, which however proper for him to utter in his day, and with the warrant of his indignation, is no longer admitted into good company, the effusion has been left out."[26]

Most often Milton's is, admittedly, "grim laughter,"[27] since he lived a life of controversy and used his wit in "Christian warfare." Wit so used is satirical: thus the two key words meet.

Aubrey brought them together long ago: "Extreme pleasant in his conversation, & at dinner, supper &c: but Satyricall. He pronounced the letter R very hard: a certain signe of a Satyricall Witt fr. Jo: Dreyden."[28] In the margin Aubrey added, "Littera canina," for that was what the Roman satirists called the letter R. "R is the *dog's* letter, and hurrieth in the sound," noted Ben Jonson in his English grammar.[29] Whatever this meant in the way of a burr,[30] he who was to be the greatest satirist of the age apprehended that it boded not well for those who might stumble across Milton's path. Of course there was hindsight, based on Milton's actual publications, to make such an inference easier. And Dryden may himself have been the victim of a pleasantry when Milton gave him permission to "tag" his lines. Certainly readers of *The State of Innocence and Fall of Man* will be inclined to think so, especially if the blank verse poet went on to say, as one version has it, "Some of 'em are so Awkward and Old Fashion'd that I think you had as good leave 'em as you found 'em."[31] It appears that more than one shot was fired in a war between these two about "the jingling sound of like endings," "the troublesome and modern bondage of rhyming," skill in which Dryden considered Milton lacking.[32]

To continue this pairing, is the line in *Mac Flecknoe* "Thy inoffensive satires never bite" (200) a reminiscence of Joseph Hall's hapless offering of "Toothlesse Satyrs" followed by "byting Satires"?[33] And if so, was Dryden inspired by Milton's merciless logic: "A toothless satyr [Milton's interesting spelling[34]] is as improper as a toothed sleekstone, and as bullish"; "For if it bite neither the persons nor the vices, how is it a satyr, and if it bite either, how is it toothless, so that toothless satyrs are as much as if he had said toothless teeth."[35] "Relics of the bum" (*Mac Flecknoe* 101) echoes a hit in *Defensio Secunda* and *Pro Se Defensio*.[36]

Keeping to English, we can compare a passage from *Of Reformation,* "I know many of those that pretend to be great rabbis in these studies have scarce saluted them from the strings, and the title-page, or to give 'em more, have been but the ferrets and mouse-hunts of an index," (*Works,* III, 35) with Pope's "How index-learning turns no student pale,/ Yet holds the eel of science by the tail" (*Dunciad* 1:280).

Dryden, Pope, even Swift: we can catch Milton and Swift saying the same thing, with the customary eighteenth-century increase in literalness. Thomas Birch put on record in 1738[37] a bon mot the authenticity of which there seems to be no reason to doubt.

> Mr. [John] *Ward* saw Mrs. [Deborah] *Clarke, Milton's* Daughter, at the House of one of her Relations, not long before her Death [in 1727], "when she informed me, says that gentleman, that she and her Sisters us'd to read to their Father in eight Languages; which by practice they were capable of doing with great readiness and accuracy, tho' they understood what they read in no other Language but *English;* and their Father us'd often to say in their hearing, *one Tongue was enough for a Woman.*"

It is a reliable line of transmission, from Milton's youngest daughter to Ward, who was professor of rhetoric in Gresham College, to Birch, a diligent gatherer of material who, the very next day after he heard this story from Ward, visited Milton's granddaughter for more information. The jest stuck in Deborah's mind some sixty years, to the end of her life. Her recollection (or Ward's) might be inaccurate on other things: for example, only one of her sisters, not both, shared the task of reading to their father; Phillips, who is more to be trusted here, says that the eldest, Anne, was excused on account of a defect. In short one can and does forget a bit of life, but not an epigram as coruscating as "One tongue is enough for a woman."

This was or became a proverb.[38] It turns up in Swift's *A Complete Collection of Genteel and Ingenious Conversation*,[39] published the same year as Birch's *Complete Collection*, 1738. Miss Notable at table says, "Pray, Mr. Nerout, will you please to send me a piece of tongue?" Is answered, "Never. By no means, madam: one tongue is enough for a woman."

A point is here made of invoking Milton's great successors in the field of devastation because, although one must distinguish between satire as a mode and satire as a form, Dryden, Pope, and Swift are granted licenses that, for three centuries, Milton has been denied. The feeling seems to be that he must not operate on any level below the grandiose. He often deviated from the sublime and solemn, and most of the time with zest and wit and high moral purpose, and we miss a great deal by refusing to look and understand. Not to quote critics who, because of their dates, can be called old-fashioned, we find the same averted gaze and wringing of hands in the general introduction to volume IV of the Yale *Complete Prose Works*.[40] Here, if anywhere, we should expect appreciation, since it is this volume that gives us for the first time proper annotations to the three *Defences*. We are put on notice that the accompanying new translations are "distinguished,"[41] but Milton as a satirist is repeatedly devalued and deplored, though *Mercurius Fumigosus* is lavishly quoted and praised,[42] Marchamont Needham approved for writing like Milton[43] (but Milton ruled out when he writes like Needham), and Sir John Birkenhead identified as "a satirist of remarkable talent and insight."[44] Let one sentence of the indictment represent the whole: "No rhetorical device in *A Defence* is more destructive to Milton's persuasiveness than his persistent use of epithets, the variety and dullness of which is astonishing in a mind so capacious."[45] The logic is equal to the grammar. Why should "variety" be "astonishing in a mind so capacious"? One would think variety would be expected of a capacious mind: and Milton gives it to us. The use of "is" instead of "are": "the variety and dullness . . . is astonishing" indicates that for the writer variety and dullness are close in meaning. Also, the descriptive "bitter" is applied four times,[46] where another perception is that Milton is enjoying himself hugely, feeling mightily within himself his resources of learning and argumentation and mockery, as he takes on, in turn, "the great Kill-cow of Christendom" (as Phillips called him[47]), Salmasius, pseudo-Morus, Morus. He was not being merely personal, at least in the first two *Defences*. As F. E. Hutchinson[48] has commented, "In some true if incomplete sense he was delivering to the world, in his first and second *Defence of the English People,* that epic 'doctrinal and exemplary to a nation,' to which he had early dedicated his powers."

To criticize a polemicist because he has "inflammatory sentences"[49] is comparable to complaining because a sonnet has fourteen lines or because blank verse does not rhyme. Happily, the editors or translators of the individual *Defences,* in their introductions, go their own way. Donald C. Mackenzie, translator of the first *Defence,* notes, "No one style, in fact, can handle the variety [here "variety" seems not to be pejorative] of styles in Milton's Latin. At times it is senatorial rhetoric, and we hear again Cicero against Catiline or Antony. At times it is Plautine comedy, earthy in its humor [the general editor had said it was "unrelieved even by humor or lightness"[50]] and delighting in puns. At times the dominant tone is the satirist's *saeva indignatio.*"[51] Donald A. Roberts calls attention to "the varied play of wit, and the rhetorical brilliance of *Defensio Secunda*" and identifies its form, "panegyric and diatribe."[52]

The following passage from Lillian Feder's article "John Dryden's Use of Classical Rhetoric"[53] fits Milton so well that we could substitute his name throughout:

> Dryden here [*A Defence of an Essay of Dramatic Poetry*] combines the image of the warrior in the chivalric trial by combat with that of the orator engaged in a verbal battle. There are interesting parallels in the writings of Cicero and Quintilian, both of whom frequently use the image of a battle or a gladiatorial con-

> test when referring to an argument in the law court or forum. Often in an extended image, combining the language of oratory with that of physical combat, they picture the orator debating *in aciem forensam*. In the same way Dryden depicts himself as the orator at arms. His cause is a good one, and, like a good orator, he must find the right arguments and their proper arrangement. Indeed, this is no mere literary dispute: it is an argument that will bring *honor* and *glory* to the winner. So significant is the contest that Dryden uses as an image the hereditary champion of England.

So we are back to Edward Phillips' language about the combat with Salmasius:[54] "There could nowhere have been found a champion that durst lift up the pen against so formidable an adversary, had not our little English David had the courage to undertake this great French Goliath." We are back to the Bohn misprint of *Areopagitica,* "sallies out and *seeks* her adversary," that so many eminent scholars and critics have followed, and ultimately they are right, for a closely parallel passage in *Pro Se Defensio* has "hostem petere.[55]

J. Milton French's theory was that Milton was divided, that he suffered a dichotomy between the poet in him and the rationalist, that, indeed, his "mind . . . was essentially critical rather than creative."[56] This can more easily be said of A. E. Housman, who wrote tender lyrics while mercilessly pillorying other scholars in his classical prefaces and reviews. It should not be possible to forget how much of Milton's poetry takes the form of debate and symbolic combat: The Lady versus Comus, the forces of good in *Paradise Lost* versus the forces of evil, Samson versus Dalila and Harapha, Jesus versus the Tempter. (Has there been any complaint that Jesus, with whom Milton probably identifies as much as with Samson, is curt rather than courteous to his opponent?) Remembering again the assailing of the bishops in "Lycidas," how far back can we go in this lifelong pattern, leaving out the scholastic exercises? "L'Allegro" versus "Il Penseroso"?

It is just possible that Milton made his debut as a polemicist with his "Paraphrase on Psalm 114," "done . . . at fifteen years old." One wonders why, of the 150 Psalms, it was Number 114 that was chosen. (Given 114, 136 will follow, for its similar theme.) True, it characteristically, prophetically, gratifyingly, sounds the note of "liberty." But in 1623 liberty from whom, from what? King James? Archbishop Abbot, who was in virtual retirement because he had killed a keeper in a hunting accident and who in any case was believed to be in sympathy with the Puritans? The clue may lie in a letter of John Chamberlain's[57] about the rejoicing of the people of London in October 1623 when Prince Charles returned from Spain without the Infanta, whom it was feared he would bring back as his Roman Catholic bride. There were bonfires in the streets, and "A number of other particulers I could set downe too long to relate, but among all there beeing solemne service in Powles the singing of a new antheme was specially observed, the 114th psalme, when Israell came out of Egipt and the house of Jacob from among the barbarous people." Thus from the St. Paul's schoolboy we could be getting something of a political allegory, like *Absalom and Achitophel*, with "Israel" meaning England in both heroic-couplet poems.

An analytical survey needs to be made of Milton's puns.[58] A very recent editor has found no less than three meanings for "peering" in "peering day," Nativity Ode 140: "appearing, scrutinizing, equalizing."[59] The last is hard to apply, but, *pace* the Columbia *Variorum Commentary*, do we need to choose between "appearing" and "scrutinizing" when both have their urgency in context?[60] How many reverberations has "hollow states" in the sonnet to Vane (cf. "hollow truce," *P.L.* 6:578)? When Camus comes "footing slow" ("Lycidas" 103), does "footing" subliminally conceal the word *pedant?*[61] Is there really a pun in *De Doctrina Christiana?*[62] Certainly this scholar is an inveterate etymologist and lexicographer, which is the apologia for "ravens . . . though ravenous" (*P.R.* 2:269). For novelty we may take a closer look at Abdiel's confrontation of Satan before smiting him with his sword. "My sect thou seest," he says (6:147). By "sect" he means "party," but may he not also mean "sword" (Latin *secare* and *sectio*, "cut")?[63]

This author's irony must never be underrated. Dalila

tells her husband she has come "to lighten what thou sufferest" (*S.A.* 744). "Lighten" is "relieve," but it also turns out to mean "make clearer."[64] A 1964 contributor to *Notes and Queries*[65] discovered "an ironic pun" in line 280 of Book 3 of *Paradise Regained,* "There Babylon the wonder of all tongues," since the longer epic (12:342-43) and Semitic authority identified Babylon with Babel. What follows the commentator fails to point out—that "the wonder of all tongues" is also "the *wounder* of all tongues,"[66] and "Babylon," of course, is "babble on"!

It took time for editors to get together on understanding that in *Areopagitica* "enchiridion"[67] is used in a double sense —a manual of devotion *and* a dagger. This is, after all, the work that De Quincey labeled "the finest specimen extant of generous scorn."[68] Therein "our London trading St. Thomas in his vestry"[69] is multileveled: (1) trading was going on within the supposedly "hallowed limits" in Cheapside; (2) it was trading in clothing: thus "vestry" is a pun; (3) the pun is strengthened by the recollection that "St. Thomas" was the older name of the Mercers' chapel (and *mercenary* is latent here: Milton launched all this with reference to the vending of sermons); (4) St. Thomas received the Virgin Mary's girdle on her Assumption; (5) Milton has been attacking the vestments of the clergy since *Of Reformation.*[70] In stride now, we next get "and add to boot St. Martin and St. Hugh," which conveys us by way of the saint who shared his cloak (and the liberty of St. Martin le Grand, where petty commerce was as rife as under the nave of St. Paul's) to the unofficial patron saint of shoemakers—from vestments to boots, sheer fun making: there was no church dedicated to St. Hugh in London.

In Latin controversy his exuberance in this kind knows no bounds. Bitter? It is hilarious. The syca*more* complex of puns is one of the most ingenious ever erected.[71] (But Milton began sporting with "moratus sum"—"I have delayed" and "I have played the fool"; to combine both meanings, a translator would have to resort to, "I've fooled around enough"—

at the end of Prolusio VI,[72] a word play that dates back to Nero, as there noted.) Where can we find a more stunning retort—literally a *twisting back*—than the transmutation of More's gibe, "Orestis aemule" ("O emulous of Orestes!"—i.e., madman) to "O restis aemule" ("O emulous of a rope!")?[73] Give a fool a little room—and he'll hang himself. Another pun involving spacing can be found in *Samson Agonistes* 235: "vanquished with a peal of words" ("a peal" meaning a volley and "appeal").

The nickname of the maid of Salmasius is altered from "Bontia" to "Pontia," because it is more fruitful that way, yielding Latin *pons,* bridge, Greek *pontus,* sea, *pontifex,* Pontius Pilate, Pontia—a woman who poisoned her children—and the region of Pontus, with its various demeaning legends. To look at a clause of multiple reference that still needs annotation, More is accused: "qui denique totam illam Pontiae Sestiada sicco pede praeterieris":[74] "you who, in fine, would pass over, with dry foot, that whole Sestiad of Pontia." In other words More is trying to skip over an amorous scandal involving himself and Pontia. He is not good at *praeteritio*—that is, he is as wretched a rhetorician as he is a man.[75] "Sestiada," a Greek accusative singular of a word that dates back to Musaeus, is an allusion to the Marlowe-Chapman poem *Hero and Leander,*[76] which is in "sestiads," a term Chapman used to refer both to Sestos, Hero's home in Thrace, and to the six parts into which he divided the poem. We have "Alexander the Phrygian" (Paris, the great lover) More crossing the Helles*pont* (was it Hell for him, after Pontia dug her nails into his face?) without getting his feet wet. (Xerxes did accomplish that, by means of pontoons.) The implication is that he would make a fitting subject for a mock epic. (Does he think he is a divinity that he can go dry-footed like Circe: "Summaque decurrit pedibus super aequora siccis"—Ovid's *Metamorphoses* 14:50. He is not like Dante's Heavenly Messenger who passed over the Styx with soles unwet, "passava Stige colle piante asciutte" [*Inferno* 9:81]. No "dear might of Him that walked the waves" ["Lycidas" 173] attends More.)

Pons asinorum! It is ridiculous, and it is as pointless to feel sorry for him as for Shadwell, but where Dryden wrote a lampoon, Milton is still out to correct and reform: besides defending himself, he is a spokesman for a side that he believes to be right. As a great critic said, "He reserved his anger for the enemies of religion, freedom, and his country."[77] As he himself said, anger *and* laughter are "those two most rational faculties of human intellect."[78]

Let us give up the old pastime of opposing Milton's left hand to his right, when the complicated truth is that he was ambidextrous, his *ingenium* a two-handed engine serving poetry and reform.

Notes

1 It has been a long while since J. Milton French's pioneering article "Milton as Satirist," *PMLA,* 51 (1936), 414-29. Since I first published in 1967, the principal articles have been T. J. B. Spencer, "Paradise Lost: The Anti-Epic," in C. A. Patrides, ed., *Approaches to "Paradise Lost"* (London, 1968), pp. 81-98, and Irene Samuel, "Milton on Comedy and Satire," *HLQ,* 35 (1972, 107-30). Spencer quotes a number of modern critics on comedy in *Paradise Lost;* Samuel, quoting ancient and Renaissance criticism (and citing no moderns except Gilbert), finds comedy and humor in the three long poems theoretically, and therefore actually, impossible. She was answered, before she wrote, by John Reesing. "The flexibility and variety of Milton's responsiveness in *Paradise Lost* have not always received their full due. For one thing, comic notes, though decorously subordinated always to more grand and epic concerns, are often firmly registered. There is a pervasive delight in puns and other forms of verbal wit, as critics have recently been noticing. There is

awareness, grim and sardonic and contained in fear, yet still genuine awareness of comic inflation in the characters of Hell. There is an attitude childlike and playful—and wistful—toward the antics of Adam and Eve's domestic zoo; in the last book there is a sense of mild and benevolent amusement at Adam's impulsiveness. There is even a sense for the comically enigmatic in the representation of the good angels looking at the new cannon, which Raphael so painstakingly describes—something of the impulse to chuckle that we manage to suppress as we watch a naive but clever child try to puzzle out a suspicious situation." *Milton's Poetic Art: "A Mask," "Lycidas," and "Paradise Lost"* (Cambridge, Mass., 1969), p. 114.

2 *The Reason of Church Government,* Columbia *Works,* III, 232.

3 "Milton in Rustication," *SP,* 19 (1922), 116.

4 Isabel G. MacCaffrey, ed., Milton's *"Samson Agonistes" and the Shorter Poems* (New York, 1966), pp. ix, xv, xxiv.

5 *The Metaphysicals and Milton* (London, 1956), pp. 61-74.

6 *The Shakespearean Moment* (New York, 1960), pp. 203ff.

7 *Milton's Minor Poems* (Pittsburgh, 1969), pp. 22-39, 57ff.

8 *SAMLA Studies in Milton,* ed. J. Max Patrick (Gainesville, 1953), "Milton's Defense of Bawdry," pp. 65f.

9 Edward Le Comte, *"Samson Agonistes* and *Aureng-Zebe," EA,* 11 (1958), 18-22; Martin A. Larson, "The Influence of Milton's Divorce Tracts on Farquhar's *Beaux Stratagem, PMLA,* 39 (1924), 174-78. In act II of *The Way of the World* Millamant's entrance is a take-off on Dalila's (*S.A.* 710ff): "Here she comes, i'faith, full sail, with her fan spread and her streamers out, and a shoal of fools for tenders."

10 But Parker (*Milton,* pp. 104-5) denies that Milton

lacked a sense of humour. On the contrary, he had a sharp satiric wit and a certain gift for burlesque; he enjoyed, and could express eloquently, the more extravagant incongruities of life. In the gusto of controversy his combative spirit could be Rabelaisian, without the grosser indecency of Rabelais. Together with a broad, heavy-handed humour, which found its most natural outlet in sarcastic parenthesis and mocking comment, his nature embraced, paradoxically, a strain of geniality and playfulness. When sure of himself and of his audience, he could indulge in light irony, touched with tenderness. Milton did not lack a sense of humour, but his sense of humour lacked range. It also lacked confidence.

This is apropos of the young man; his confidence grew.

11 *Complete Poetical Works,* ad loc.

12 Parker, *Milton's Contemporary Reputation,* (Columbia, 1940), p. 107. French, *Life Records,* IV, 358, translates "Aberwitz" as "craziness"; it is, rather, "false strained wit."

13 *Animadversions, Works,* III, 143.

14 Thomas Kranidas, *The Fierce Equation: A Study of Milton's Decorum* (The Hague, 1965), p. 143.

15 Ibid., pp. 150, 144, 153, 154. Kranidas's remarks are very different from Gregory Ziegelmaier's, "The Comedy of *Paradise Lost,*" *College English,* 26 (1965), 516-22, which, dwelling on the "cosmic laughter" or "divine humor," is depressingly reminiscent of Dr. Johnson's famous review of Soame Jenyns's *Free Enquiry into the Nature and Origin of Evil* (in Johnson's *Works* [Oxford, 1825], VI, 47ff.

16 *Answerable Style* (Minneapolis, 1953), pp. 17-37.

17 What has been the most widely used college text, Merritt Y. Hughes's edition of the *Complete Poetry and Major Prose* (New York, 1957), has dropped the note to 1. 91 that was in the same editor's *"Paradise Regained," The Minor Poems, and "Samson Agonistes"* (New York, 1937), p. 116.

18 *Oliver's Secretary* (New York), p. 15.

19 Ibid., p. 12.

20 *Milton* (New York, 1967), p. 119. G. M. Trevelyan called it "a jesting sonnet" (*England under the Stuarts* [London, 1947], p. 197). See further Columbia *Variorum Commentary,* II, 374-75.

21 Tillyard, *Milton,* p. 253.

22 Tillyard, *The Miltonic Setting* (London, 1938), pp. 1-28.

23 Tillyard, *Studies in Milton* (New York, 1951), p. 74.

24 Milton, *Private Correspondence and Academic Exercises,* tr. Phyllis B. Tillyard (Cambridge, 1932), p. 94. She also does not locate the lice, p. 97: cf. *Works,* XII, 236.

25 Dd. 6.30.P.22v.

26 J. A. Wittreich, Jr., *The Romantics on Milton* (Cleve-

land, 1970), p. 450.

27 *Animadversions, Works,* III, 107.

28 Darbishire, *Early Lives,* p. 6.

29 *Works,* ed. William Gifford (Boston 1853), p. 899.

30 Probably the idiosyncrasy was most noticeable with preconsonantal *r,* which in London was on its modern way out; Milton was again being old-fashioned. Cf. Helge Kökeritz, *Shakespeare's Pronunciation* (New Haven, 1953), p. 315. E. J. Dobson concludes: "His pronunciation of the short vowels, especially before *r,* was somewhat conservative, even as compared, in one respect or another, with Daines, Hodges, and Wallis, and certainly as compared with the younger writers after 1670. This must be reckoned the most individual characteristic of his speech, and must be associated with his 'hard' [*r*] on which Aubrey remarked; one may imagine him as resembling, in these respects, a modern Scottish speaker." "Milton's Pronunciation," *Language and Style in Milton,* ed. Ronald D. Emma and John T. Shawcross (New York, 1967), p. 188.

31 Darbishire, p. 335.

32 Masson, *Life of Milton,* VI (London, 1880), 633ff.; Morris Freedman, "Milton and Dryden on Rhyme," *HLQ,* 24 (1961), 337-44.

33 Dryden's *Poetical Works,* ed. George R. Noyes (Boston, 1950), p. 1060.

34 "The derivation of satire from Greek satyr rather than Roman *satura,* a common confusion, gives Milton his running pun: A toothless satyr would be a feeble old satyr indeed." Samuel, p. 116.

35 *Animadversions, Works,* III, 114; *An Apology,* III, 329.

36 *Works,* VIII, 176; IX, 172. Anne Davidson Ferry's *Milton and the Miltonic Dryden* (Cambridge, Mass., 1968) says nothing about the satiric connection between the two authors.

37 Ed. *A Complete Collection of the Historical, Political, and Miscellaneous Works of John Milton* (London), I, lxi-ii.

38 Morris Palmer Tilley, *A Dictionary of the Proverbs in England in the Sixteenth and Seventeenth Centuries* (Ann Arbor, 1950), p. 675 (T 398).

39 In *A Tale of a Tub, The Battle of the Books, and Other Satires,* (Everyman's Library), p. 299.

40 Ed. Don M. Wolfe (New Haven, 1966).

41 Ibid., pp. 102, 109 (footnotes).

42 Ibid., pp. 203ff.

43 Ibid., pp. 49ff, 124.

44 Ibid., p. 207.

45 Ibid., p. 114.

46 Ibid., pp. 109, 231, 252, 257.

47 Darbishire, p. 70.

48 *Milton and the English Mind* (London, 1946), p. 84. Cf. the reference above, p. 89, n. 1.

49 Yale *Prose Works,* IV, 91.

50 Ibid., p. 112.

51 Ibid., p. 296.

52 Ibid., pp. 538, 540. One of the contributors to IV says of the two contributors to V: "They are fortunate in the fact that their volume is not encumbered with a long and often irrelevant introduction by another hand. . . ." *RQ,* 26 (1973), 91.

53 *PMLA,* 69 (1954), 1262 (see n. 9 there for full references).

54 Darbishire, p. 70.

55 *Works,* IX, 224. See above, pp. 86, 96, n. 69, and my *Milton Dictionary* (New York, 1961), s.v. "Bohn edition." Besides following in the classical tradition of adversary oratory, Milton is in the line of the flytings of the humanists. Charles Nisard's *Les Gladiateurs de la république des lettres aux XVe, XVIe et XVIIe Siècles* (Paris, 1860), which does not mention him, illustrates his techniques in detail. Since a professor has defended George Herbert's pattern poems on the ground that he was not the first to do them, it may be comforting to know that Milton was not the first to call an opponent a "Pork" (*Colasterion, Works,* IV, 250): Poggio had called Filelfo that (Nisard, p. 127). Whatever we think of the answer "Ha, ha, ha" (*Animadversions, Works,* III, 170), it is not peculiar to Milton: it can be found before him (*The Marprelate Tracts* [1588-89], ed. William Pierce, London, 1911, p. 32) and after him (*The Man in the Moon,* quoted—without this connection—in Yale *Prose Works,* IV, 18). Sir Thomas More's name had been made free with, by his enemies

as well as by his friends, a point with which Alexander More consoled himself early in his *Fides Publica.*

56 "Milton as a Historian," *PMLA,* 50 (1935), 476.

57 *Letters,* ed. Norman E. McClure (Philadelphia, 1939), II, 516.

58 I do not mean that the subject has not often been touched on, usually in deprecation. There are some quotations from commentators, a brief bibliography, and acute original comments in the "Word-Play" section of *Milton's Grand Style* by Christopher Ricks (Oxford, 1963), pp. 66-75: cf. p. 15. James Brown reaps much from "fruitless embraces" (*P.L.* 5:215), pp. 16-17 and 25 of "Eight Types of Puns, *PMLA,* 71 (1956).

59 John T. Shawcross, ed., *The Complete Poetry* (New York, 1971), p. 68. "Seems forced," says *MQ,* 6 (1972), 100, of "equalizing."

60 The *Variorum Commentary,* II, 641-42 (New York, 1972), points to three significations of "dear" at "Lycidas" 6. Jon S. Lawry, *The Shadow of Heaven: Matter and Stance in Milton's Poetry* (Ithaca, 1968), finds double meanings in "live" (L'Allegro" 152) and "Heav'n" (*Comus* 777), pp. 47, 88.

61 J. Mitchell More, "A Pun in 'Lycidas,' " *NQ,* n.s. 5 (1958), 211. Bush comments (*Variorum Commentary,* II, 671): "While Milton, especially in prose, could make Joycean puns, this one would seem to be quite out of key" (presumably St. Peter's key!). Students of mine have uncovered sensational topical allusions. Since L'Allegro admits to enjoying Shakespeare on "the well-trod stage," "Sometimes with secure delight, / The upland Hamlets will invite" (lines 91-92) refers to provincial productions of the Bard's best-known play (Wesley Romansky). As regards the commencement of the pastoral allegory in "Lycidas," one should be alert for a reference to bishops, and there it is—"Together both, ere the high lawns appeared" (25), "a lawny resemblance" (*Reason of Church Government, Works,* III, 268) that comes to full pomp with: "They would request us to endure still the rustling of their silken cassocks, and that we would burst our midriffs, rather than laugh to see them under sail in all their lawn and sarcenet, their shrouds and tackle, with a geometrical rhomboides upon their heads" (to make the proud high lawns still higher) (*Of Reformation, Works,* III, 74) (Harry Weintraub). I myself must confess that, powerfully struck by the

resemblance to *Samson Agonistes* of lines 410-15 of Book 1 of *Paradise Regained,* I get an uncanny feeling that in line 414, "Ejected, emptied, gazed, unpitied, shunned," "Gaza" is in the background of "gazed." This would be on the edge of consciousness, like some matters brought up in my *Areopagitica* essay. Robert R. Cawley noted, in an unexpected place *(Milton's Literary Craftsmanship: A Study of "A Brief History of Moscovia"* [Princeton, 1941], p. 40), "In a mind like Milton's the subconscious was always strongly operative and would be certain to color whatever he wrote." On the other hand fine critics have printed suggestions I cannot credit—e.g., that "courtly stable" at the end of the Nativity Ode (243) offers "transverse puns on courtliness and stability." Lawry, p. 39 n.; Diaches, *Milton,* p. 48. *Chacun à son espirit!* Of the perhaps startlingly sexual lines in *Comus,* "Next this marble venom'd seat / Smeared with gumms of glutenous heat / I touch with chaste palms moist and cold" (915-17), it has been asked, "Is Milton punning on the word *gluteus,* buttock?" J. W. Flosdorf, *MQ,* 7 (1973), 5.

62 See above, p. 82.

63 This is the etymology given by the Funk and Wagnalls *New Standard Dictionary of the English Language* (New York, 1929). Most dictionaries favor an ultimate derivation from *sequi,* "follow," but what Milton thought the derivation was, and whether he was right (he was wrong about "ravens"—"ravenous") have little or no bearing on the possibility of word play. The usage I propose would come under 6b of the *OED,* "with pseudo-etymological reference."

64 Cf. Lawrence W. Hyman, *The Quarrel Within: Art and Morality in Milton's Poetry* (Port Washington, New York, 1972), p. 104.

65N.s. 11, 337: John E. Parish, "An Unrecognized Pun in *Paradise Regained.*"

66 Compare Hamlet's "wonder-wounded hearers" (V.i. 280). I suspect there is the same pun in I *Henry VI IV,* vii.48, the Bastard's couplet, "Hew them to pieces, hack their bones asunder, / Whose life was England's glory, Gallia's wonder." It is true that Milton in his youth rhymed "wound" with "ground" (*Comus* 1000-01), but this was a "common variant pronunciation" (Dobson, p. 175), not the main one. The spelling was often identical.

67 *Works,* IV, 329.

68 Wittreich, p. 469.

69 *Works,* IV, 335.

70 If not, after all, "Lycidas"—see n. 61 above.

71 *Defensio Secunda, Works,* VIII, 32.

72 *Works,* XII, 246.

73 Columbia *Works* treats this spacing as a typographical error: IX, 304. Let us hope not, even though there is an undoubted slip (of the same kind) two words before. Puns are aural: Milton was in his element, alert for the kill. A further development is the syntactical pun: "A fairer person lost not Heaven" (*P.L.* 2:110), "an ambiguous arrangement of words that can be thought in both directions." Reesing, p. 56.

74 *Pro Se Defensio, Works,* IX, 188.

75 The style is the man. "Milton believed that the vicious attitudes of his eminent adversaries could best be exposed through their own language." D. M. Rosenberg, "Parody of Style in Milton's Polemics," *Milton Studies,* 2, 1970 (Pittsburgh), 113.

76 It is first an allusion to Musaeus's *Hero and Leander,* but that Milton has English literature on his mind is shown by his reference in the next clause to *Romeo and Juliet,* for so I have taken "Tibaltianam"—in a context of love and quarreling—to be. Records have been searched in vain for a girl of that name. Perhaps a better candidate is the Tybalt of Sir William Davenant's epic *Gondibert* (1651), a lover as well as a knight. Interestingly enough, *Gondibert* has a phrase from *Areopagitica,* "cloyster'd vertue" (1:1:74). Alexander Chalmers, ed., *Works of the English Poets* (London, n.d.), VI, 377.

77 Coleridge in Wittreich, p. 218.

78 *Animadversions, Works,* III, 108.

INDEX